A photo of Nico appeared on the screen. Standing in a kitchen, smiling at the photographer. Her. He'd been smiling at her.

His entire face was lit up, his brown eyes focused entirely on her.

This photo.

Freya could fall asleep looking at that photo.

But had she?

He's always been great to you. I've always wondered why you two aren't together.

She'd been wondering the same thing. The more she got to know him, the more she liked him. She was attracted to him, had been from the start. Surely London Freya must have been too. And if thirty-year-old Freya was falling for him as a stranger, wouldn't twenty-five-year-old Freya have as well?

"We work together. We're friends." It seemed like a plausible explanation to Freya. It was what everyone else believed, but did she?

Dear Reader,

Thank you for picking up a copy of *Italian Tycoon to Remember*.

Friends to lovers is one of my favorite tropes, but it's so hard to write, because if a couple is meant to be, whatever is stopping them from being together must be pretty big, right?

I cheated a little in Freya and Nico's case. It's difficult to know your best friend is "the one" if you have no memories of him at all. Freya is in an accident, and when she wakes, everything in her life is different: her job, her roommate, even the continent she lives on.

Nico is carrying so much guilt around with him it's a wonder he can even stand, and suddenly it isn't clear whether these best friends will find their HEA.

I had such a wonderful time writing their story and reliving my recent unforgettable trip to Italy.

I hope you enjoy Freya and Nico's story.

Justine xx

ITALIAN TYCOON TO REMEMBER

JUSTINE LEWIS

Recycling programs for this product may not exist in your area.

ISBN-13: 978-1-335-47058-4

Italian Tycoon to Remember

For questions and comments about the quality of this book, please contact us at CustomerService@Harlequin.com.

Harlequin Enterprises ULC
22 Adelaide St. West, 41st Floor
Toronto, Ontario M5H 4E3, Canada
www.Harlequin.com

HarperCollins Publishers
Macken House, 39/40 Mayor Street Uppe
Dublin 1, D01 C9W8, Ireland
www.HarperCollins.com

Printed in U.S.A.

Justine Lewis writes uplifting, heartwarming contemporary romances. She lives in Australia with her hero husband, two teenagers and an outgoing puppy. When she isn't writing, she loves to walk her dog in the bush near her house, attempt to keep her garden alive and search for the perfect frock. She loves hearing from readers, and you can visit her at justinelewis.com.

Books by Justine Lewis

Harlequin Romance

If the Fairy Tale Fits...

Beauty and the Playboy Prince

Invitation from Bali

Breaking the Best Friend Rule
The Billionaire's Plus-One Deal

Princesses' Night Out

How to Win Back a Royal

Summer Escapes

Dating Game with Her Enemy

Billionaire's Snowbound Marriage Reunion
Fiji Escape with Her Boss
Back in the Greek Tycoon's World
Swipe Right for Mr. Perfect

Visit the Author Profile page at Harlequin.com.

For Peter, who is unforgettable

Praise for
Justine Lewis

"Justine Lewis will capture every reader's heart with her poignant, intense and dramatic contemporary romance, *Billionaire's Snowbound Marriage Reunion*. A beautifully written tale...this affecting romantic read will move readers to tears and have them falling in love with both Lily and Jack."

—*Goodreads*

CHAPTER ONE

The rehabilitation ward was much quieter than the neurology ward. There was no constant beeping, no clinking trolleys, no one entering her room at all hours to take endless observations. Freya had finally been able to get a proper night's sleep and she felt better than she had since the accident. Her physical injuries were superficial: a bruise on her cheekbone that was fading, cuts on her right arm and hand that were bandaged and stiff but not troubling her.

She almost felt normal.

Except she wasn't.

Not a bit.

There were many things bothering her, but they all came back to one single problem.

The day's date.

Though the date only seemed to be a problem for her—everyone else in the world was completely fine with it. But then, they could remember the last five years of their lives.

'There's someone here to see you, Freya,' the nurse said, knocking on the door frame.

Feeling well, simply confused, Freya was out of bed and sitting in the armchair by the window of her single room looking out at an unfamiliar London street.

A tall, broad-shouldered man walked in. He had hair as brown as it could be without being black and a strong, definitive jawline. She couldn't make out the colour of his eyes, which wouldn't meet hers, but she remembered him from a few days ago. He'd been amongst the doctors and the nurses in her room when she'd first woken up. He had the kind of good looks that caught in your throat and upset your ability to breathe. He hadn't even spoken, but had still stood out from the rest of the medical professionals crowding into her room.

Her heart still fell when she recognised him. As gorgeous as he was, rather than recognising the face of a random doctor, she'd prefer to remember what she'd been doing for the last five years.

The man wore a blue business shirt, slim fitting but not tight. Just snug enough for her to be able to see he was in pretty good shape compared to the other doctors who'd been through her room over the past week.

'Hello,' she said.

'Hello,' he replied with a smile that she almost might've described as shy.

Neither of them said anything. He seemed to be waiting for her to speak first, but what was she supposed to say? He was the doctor. She was the amnesia patient. She didn't have any answers. Only a million questions.

'So what have you come to investigate?' she asked.

'What do you mean?'

'What's your specialty, Doctor?'

His brow furrowed and she was sorry. Nothing should ever crease a forehead as smooth as his. His face should be on a National Treasure register to keep it preserved for future generations to admire. Yet he frowned.

'I've seen the physician, the neurologist, the occupational therapist. Oh, goodness! You're the psychiatrist, aren't you? Or the psychologist?'

He winced.

'Oh, heck, I'm sorry. I know I should know the difference, and I do. Really. But I've just had a big bump on the head.' She smiled, so he'd know she was kidding. Amnesia humour. One good thing about having amnesia, and there weren't many, was that you could pretend to have forgotten things you'd never been sure about in the first place.

Still he didn't speak. He just looked at her with his big eyes. She now saw they were dark, a deep, delicious brown. She ran her tongue around her mouth, which was suddenly very dry.

'So?' she asked

'So?' he replied.

She had amnesia! Could he be a bit less judgemental?

'It's one of the two, isn't it? One of the headshrinkers. Sorry, I'm probably not allowed to say that either. I don't know what words are acceptable five years in the future. But that's why you're making me do all the talking, isn't it? You want to analyse me.'

The man looked down and she took that as a yes. She really did want to talk to someone, try to make sense of what was happening to her.

'I guess I feel as happy as you can be when you've lost five years of memory. Five years of my life. I'm happy to be alive—don't get me wrong—but I'm also so frustrated and I think that's understandable. I'm allowed to be a bit upset, don't you think? How would you feel if you woke up five years in the future?'

'I'd be confused. Upset.'

'Yeah, and now imagine you live, not just in a different house, but in a different city. In a different country! And you're apparently a food stylist but you have absolutely no idea what a food stylist does. The last thing you remember is being sacked from your job as a photographer for a second-rate local newspaper in Pasadena, halfway around the world.'

The man looked around the room. After spying

a plastic chair next to the bed, he sat. He crossed his legs and leaned forward, resting his chin in his hand. His large, smooth, tanned hand. Psychiatrists were the doctors, right? Psychologists were the counsellors. She'd seen a psychologist once, after her father had passed away. But he'd been nowhere near as gorgeous as this semisilent man sitting in front of her now.

Which type was he? She wasn't getting a strong vibe either way, but he was definitely one or the other judging by the way he just sat there, looking at her and waiting for her to fill the silence with her babble.

'And imagine you don't know any of your friends' names. Or your colleagues. Or your housemate, who apparently is also your boss.'

At this point, she would not even have bet money on the fact that her name was Freya McFadden. And that would have been sensible since her current financial position was also a complete unknown. In the States, she'd had few savings, probably enough for a plane ticket to the UK. She'd been working here in London, but who knew how much food stylists earned? Or how much her boss was charging her for rent. She didn't know a lot about London, but she did know it was hardly a budget-friendly city.

The hospital and rehabilitation ward were quite nice, which meant she wasn't destitute. But she had nothing to compare it with. She'd never been on a rehabilitation ward in any hospital before.

'So you probably want to know what I remember.' she said.

'It would help.' His voice was high, pained.

Her last memory had been of the night of her twenty-fifth birthday. She'd been out for drinks with her best friend, Jane, drowning her sorrows after being sacked that very day.

'Who sacks someone on their birthday?' she'd cried.

Her horrible boss had told her that her work lacked vibrancy. That it wasn't dynamic enough. That *she* wasn't dynamic enough. And then she'd remembered the words her recent ex, Lachlan, had said to her not two weeks earlier, that he needed to be with someone with more 'energy.'

'Energy?' she'd moaned to Jane. 'I don't lack energy. Or vibrancy. What is that code for? What are they trying to tell me? What's wrong with me?'

Jane had shaken her head, ordered them another round of cocktails and the next thing Freya knew she'd woken up in a hospital bed in London.

'As far as I remember, I live in a share flat in the sketchy part of Pasadena with my friend Jane. I work as a photographer at a small local newspaper. At least I did until I was sacked. I have a small group of friends who I've known more than half my life. I have lunch with my mother each Sunday.'

It was the same response she'd given for the past week and was still the wrong answer. Because she didn't live in Pasadena anymore; she lived in London. She hadn't worked at the paper for almost five years.

Her mother, Jillian, had flown straight to London after the accident and tried to fill in the gaps: the day after her twenty-fifth birthday Freya had bought a one-way ticket to London. It had been an impulsive decision, sparked by frustration and heartache, but her gamble had paid off. She'd found a job she loved and a nice group of friends. But for some reason, the knock she'd had on the head had made her forget everything that had happened after leaving Pasadena. What had happened to her in London? Why had her brain decided it was best left forgotten?

As best she could, Jillian had told Freya about her London life: Freya worked for Niccolò Rossetti, a celebrity chef Freya had never heard of, and she lived with him too. Jillian told Freya she had answered an ad for a food photographer and, amazingly, had got the job. She'd been working for Niccolò for almost five years and seen his career progress from strength to strength, prestigious award to prestigious award. She had worked for him as he had gone from having one restaurant in Chelsea to three across London, alongside million-pound book deals and tours around Europe, the United States and Australia.

The sort of experiences it would have been nice to remember, Freya thought bitterly.

'Your memory will return,' Jillian said for the hundredth time as she squeezed Freya's hand.

But her mother had just been saying that to comfort them both. As the days passed, the looks on the faces of the doctors were becoming increasingly worried. The look of harrowing concern creasing the face of Dr Handsome sitting across from her now made her wrap her arms tightly around herself. What if she never got those memories back?

Freya looked down. She was wearing a pair of lovely brushed-cotton pyjamas, patterned with soft pink flowers. They were apparently hers, taken from the wardrobe in the bedroom she couldn't remember. They were gorgeous, but twenty-five-year-old Freya had never owned such things.

Dr Handsome was still watching her, still using some psychiatric trick of waiting for the patient to speak first. She obliged.

'The last thing I remember is drinking cocktails and crying because I'd been sacked. The next thing I know I'm here in the hospital and you and all the other doctors are studying me.'

And she had no idea what had become of her friend Jane after that night and her mother had told her they were no longer close. But her mother was talking about a different Freya, a Freya who had had five years to build and get used to this new life.

Dr Handsome put his ridiculously attractive face in his hands, rubbed it vigorously and let out a soft, pained moan. Somehow, she felt his pain in her own chest and tried harder, for his sake, to try to remember something. So much for putting your patient at ease.

'They say I work for this celebrity chef named Niccolò Rossetti. I haven't heard of him but he mustn't be too bad because apparently I live with him too.'

Her mother had told her that she lived in Rossetti's attic. But what did that mean? Were they friends? Did they hang out? Did she like him? Her mother told her they were good friends. But what *sort* of good friends? He hadn't been to visit her.

This doctor wasn't helping at all. Wasn't he supposed to know the right questions to ask her?

'I don't live with him, *with* him, but in his attic, which sounds a bit dark, don't you think? A little bit Jane Eyre?'

'I'm sure it's a very light, bright attic,' Dr Handsome said.

'Are you? Really? The only attics I've known have been for storage. They are for insulation and besides, it would be too hot.' She really was rambling now.

The doctor raised a perfect dark eyebrow and one corner of his mouth twitched. He actually had a lovely mouth. Pink and soft looking. Kissable.

Gah.

She was mixed up enough in the head without lusting after the gorgeous shrink. Wasn't there some name for the syndrome involving falling for your psychologist? Of course, if there was, she couldn't remember it. And she didn't need another diagnosis on top of everything else.

'Anyway, I think I'm glad I came here, I just wish I could remember it.'

The outline of the last five years was there, but it was far from coloured in. She knew facts, but not feelings. In particular, did she *like* her job? Did she *like* her boss? She supposed she must if they lived together. And besides, it didn't matter what people told her; it wasn't the same. It was like hearing a story that had happened to someone else. Glamorous job, trips to New York and Paris. It sounded great, but she was jealous of the woman it had all happened to because it just wasn't her.

'Freya, there's something I should—'

'I'm trying, I am. Really. But it's hard, especially being stuck here. I look out the window and it's so strange. I don't know this city. It's like I've just stepped off the plane.'

'You want to leave the hospital?' he asked.

'Yes,' she quickly added. 'But also no.' Because

the thought of going out into London, into her other life, was terrifying.

His eyebrow did that sexy smirk-grin thing. Was he married? He was bound to be. Was that something she could just ask?

'I want to leave, because it's stifling being here. But I'm also afraid. I don't know London. I don't know my boss. I don't even know how to do my job. I mean, what does a food stylist even do? I don't have the first idea! And how pretentious do you think the average celebrity chef is? I don't know what to say to him, how to act. Do you know any celebrity chefs? Since when was that a job description? Do you think that's what's written on his passport?'

The man tilted his head and regarded her. No doubt reaching some conclusion about how messed up she was. Strangely with this doctor, she didn't feel worried; for the first time she felt as though she could say all her fears aloud. There was something about him that made her comfortable. But also, truth be told, more than a little excited. Alive.

And being alive was good. Notwithstanding the black hole that was her memory, she was immensely glad to be here, living and breathing, and that she hadn't perished in the car accident.

She leaned forward. 'Can I ask you something?'

He didn't respond. No words. And not the eyebrow thing either. She took that as permission.

'Doctor, it's none of my business, but are you married?'

He coughed. The cough turned into a choke. She scrambled around for some water to offer him.

He waved her away and composed himself. 'I'm not a doctor.'

'Oh.' Then who the heck was he? 'What do you do?'

'My passport says chef.'

'Oh.'

'But I guess people do sometime add "celebrity" to the front.' He grinned, but the grin had a hint of a grimace.

Of course.

She remembered with blinding clarity how her mouth had never been too small for her foot to fit in. It was bad enough she felt terrified about meeting the Niccolò Rossetti; now she had to blurt all her fears out to him.

He knows you.

The voice in her head telling her that was fainter than a whisper.

He knows you can sometimes put your foot in your mouth. He also knows you can sometimes talk without thinking. But he must also know that you are kind and loyal and hardworking.

'Ah…'

'Freya.'

The way he said her name felt like chocolate melting in her mouth.

And if he didn't know her before, he surely did now after she'd blurted out all her thoughts and fears.

'I'm so sorry. Niccolò, isn't it?'

He nodded. She wasn't sure if she wanted him to speak or not; she longed to hear his voice and know what he was thinking but each time he spoke her insides quivered. And the way he looked at her wordlessly made her sad. Like he was confused. Angry. Disappointed.

'But you call me Nico.'

Nico. And there was that melty-heart feeling again. Nico sounded so familiar.

He doesn't mind—he knows you.

But she didn't know him.

'I really am sorry. I can't help it. It feels as though I've been dumped in someone else's life.'

'*You* don't have to be sorry.'

Why did he emphasise 'you'?

'No, I do and I am. You know me, but I don't remember you. And I wish I did. And you're my boss so I was just so rude. I'm sorry about the remarks before. I really am.'

She couldn't remember Niccolò, though the rude things she'd said to him not moments ago were seared on her brain.

She had so many questions about her life in London but she could hardly ask the man sitting before her with a slightly stern look in his eyes, even if they did know one another. There was still a wall between them. It was invisible, glasslike, but definitely there in the way he held himself aloof, the way he had hardly smiled. The way he pursed his beautiful lips together until they were white.

She was saved by a knock at the door.

An older man, wearing a bow tie and a tweed jacket, knocked at the door.

'Hello, Freya. I'm Dr Jamal.'

'Doctor?'

'Yes, I'm your neurologist.'

'Really?'

Dr Jamal looked familiar but she still glanced to Niccolò for confirmation, though she didn't know why.

'Yes, this is Dr Jamal.' Niccolò nodded.

'How are you doing today?'

Freya lifted her hands in a shrug.

'So nothing is clearer?'

She shook her head. 'My mother came this morning with her laptop and we flicked through photos. But almost all the photos Mum has are of my childhood, which I remember perfectly.' The taste of Nan's roast lamb, the bright purple of the hydrangeas in her garden. The smell of her father's aftershave. The sensation of their dog licking her toes. Those memories made water well in her eyes. She sniffed and swallowed them down.

She had yet to see any photos of her life in London. Her late twenties should be the most exciting time of her life and all she had were the recollections of others.

'I wish I could have forgotten the years from twelve to seventeen instead,' she grumbled. 'Puberty, acne and school. Why couldn't I forget *those* five years?'

The doctor laughed but Niccolò rubbed his forehead as though he was in pain.

'I think the best thing now is for you to go home. Ninety percent of traumatic amnesia patients will recover their memories within two weeks, and most will recover it within days of returning home.'

'Home? To California?'

'No. I mean Islington. But of course if you want to go back to the States we can get you in touch with the appropriate specialists. But…'

Dr Jamal looked to Niccolò and Niccolò shook his head. The doctor's forehead creased but he turned back to Freya.

'We find that most amnesia patients experience the return of their memory within days of going back to the place they are currently living. I worry that if you travel back to the United States before your memories of London have returned that the memories of your London life will remain forever blurred and confused. I would strongly advise you to return home with Mr Rossetti and check in with me in a few days' time.'

She had only met Dr Jamal a few times that she remembered, but she trusted him. Though she wasn't yet sure about Niccolò.

'Your paperwork is finalised and I believe Mr Rossetti is able to take you.'

She looked to Niccolò. Her boss. Her landlord. Stranger. She longed to go back to Pasadena. To everything and everyone she knew.

She was missing huge gaps of her memory here, but her life in Pasadena had not felt complete either.

Twenty-five-year-old Freya had climbed on a plane and travelled halfway around the world. She'd got a job with Niccolò and she'd stayed.

You have to trust that Freya. You have to trust yourself.

Besides, thirty-year-old Freya worked for a celebrity, lived in London and travelled the world. She was having the time of her life as a food stylist.

Whatever the heck that it was.

Jillian McFadden came back to the hospital shortly afterwards to help Freya pack up the few belongings she had with her. Jillian also brought a small bag with other clothes for Freya to change into. Clothes Freya didn't recognise. Not only were fashions slightly different five years in the future, but it seemed that her style had changed as well.

Back home, if she wasn't working, she'd wear jeans and T-shirts. Short skirts and tank tops. Her London wardrobe, or what she'd seen of it, was more sophisticated.

She put on a pair of soft but tailored navy pants and a bright pink sweater for the trip back to Niccolò's house. She couldn't quite bring herself to call it home.

When you get there, you're bound to start recognising things.

This also scared her. What if she didn't like the life she'd made her herself in London? What if she didn't like Niccolò? He wasn't giving off 'best-friend vibes' but rather 'aloof-boss energy.'

Freya followed her mother out of the hospital and onto a London street.

'Where are we?'

'University of London Hospital. Bloomsbury.'

The stone buildings around her were impressive, imposing. The roads were narrower than at home, frantic with cars and red buses that looked like they were out of a postcard. The street signs were different and so was the smell. It wasn't unpleasant, just different.

'And where…where do I live?'

Jillian took her hand. 'It's a beautiful house. In Islington.'

Islington. Was that in Monopoly?

'Have you been there?'

'I've been staying there.'

'You have?'

'Yes, and it's lovely.'

Her mother hailed a black cab as though she'd done it all her life and yet again Freya felt as though she was in a dream. She climbed in, expecting to be seated behind the driver, but of course she was not.

'They drive on the left here,' she muttered to herself.

Freya sat back and watched the unfamiliar streets zoom past. She'd hoped that as they got closer to the address her mother had given to the driver, she would remember, but nothing looked familiar. Surely she had driven along these roads many times, walked these sidewalks, but she remembered nothing. She felt like a tourist.

Not exactly like a tourist. Even a tourist who had mislaid their map was probably not feeling this confused.

Her stomach twisted tighter, anticipating arriving at her home. The one she shared with Niccolò. Nico. The handsome man who was not a doctor. Her cheeks burnt again, remembering anew her embarrassment at mistaking him for a doctor and for mocking his profession. To be fair, she'd also mocked her own, but that gave her little comfort.

She pressed her damp palms against her soft trousers. Navy blue and well made. Better quality than anything she'd worn at home in California. Was thirty-year-old Freya as attracted to Nico as Amnesia Freya was? Surely not. Otherwise, she would've been lusting after him for the past five years.

Or…

Could they…had they…? Was there something physical between them?

She dismissed the thought as soon as it arose. Someone would have told her if they had a relationship. Besides, she'd have remembered something like that, wouldn't she?

Why, when you don't remember anything else?

The cab stopped outside a house on a quiet road, just a street back from a canal. Jillian was right; Niccolò's house was lovely.

With a white facade and two columns by the door, it looked like a fancier version of many of the houses they had just driven past. Something rose up inside her; not memory, but expectation. This was her home!

They climbed out of the cab and Jillian took out some keys.

'Nico's at work but he said to say he'll be home later. He wanted to give you some space,' her mother explained.

Freya nodded. She was grateful for that.

You can move out, you know. Go back to Pasadena with Mum.

She could, but remembered the doctor's words:

her memories of the past five years were more likely to come back if she stayed in London, at least for the next while. However the desire to avoid all of this strangeness was pulling her towards the airport.

'Do you really have to leave?' Freya asked as Jillian unlocked the front door.

Jillian frowned.

'I'm sorry, forget I asked.'

Jillian's trip to London at short notice after Freya's accident had already left a big gap back in Pasadena. Freya's ninety-five-year-old grandfather was ailing and her mother was his main carer.

'I'll stay if you need me,' Jillian said. 'But I think in the next day or so, things will start to become clearer.'

'How about I come back with you? I don't belong here.'

'You know what the doctor said. Coming home now, before your memory's returned, won't help your recovery. Besides, sweetheart, you're building a career here. You're happy, successful.'

'I could be those things back in the States.'

'Come on inside. I bet it'll all start to make sense.'

Freya took a deep breath and followed her mother through the heavy black door. She noticed the smell first. It was familiar, but then again this was her home and her mother was standing next to her. Yet it was more than that. Excitement sparked inside her. Her memories were coming back!

But when she stepped into the hallway, she got a jolt. Because nothing was familiar. It was beautiful, more beautiful than any place she ever imagined herself living, but it was not familiar.

To her left was a wide doorway, leading to a bright living room, furnished with soft fabrics and pastels. It looked comfy and inviting.

Freya, still clutching her bag, followed her mother down a wide hallway, lined on one side with floor-to-ceiling bookshelves, and into the kitchen and another living space.

Freya gasped. The room was gorgeous. It managed to be modern yet comfortable and traditional as well. Wooden benches, cupboards of pale blue, open spaces with bright prints covering the walls and the largest stovetop she'd ever seen. The room opened to a small garden, bursting with greenery.

'Wow!' she whispered.

'It's lovely, isn't it? You both renovated the place together when you moved in.'

'Together?'

'Well, yes, but I think he left many of the decisions to you.'

Weird. So weird. But it explained why she loved the house so much. Why it was to her taste.

'Come upstairs,' Jillian said, looking at the bag Freya was holding close to her body.

Her chest was tight as she climbed the stairs, that were covered in a thick, luxurious white carpet.

Expensive. This place is expensive.

She paused at the first-floor landing.

'Nico's room is that one and I'm in here.' Jillian pointed to a room to the left.

Freya glanced to the left, resisted the urge to look into Nico's room. 'I'm in the attic, aren't I?' She began to climb the stairs.

Her room was an attic in name only. It was hardly the dusty cramped space of fairytales, but was instead filled with light. Slanted windows that faced the sky were ajar to let the fresh spring air in. There was a spectacular view over nearby gardens and rooftops. If she'd had a pick of all the rooms in the house, she would have chosen this one. London looked magical from this angle. A door led to a bathroom, large enough for a claw-foot tub. Another door led to a small room or a large walk-in closet, depending on your perspective.

'The whole floor is yours.'

The bed was covered with a floral bedspread, but with a modern pattern. She loved it. It looked like something she might have chosen and yet…

Disappointment tasted bitter on her tongue and she held back some tears.

'Are you okay? Are you remembering something?' Jillian rubbed Freya's shoulder.

Freya shook her head.

Nothing.

She'd been hoping that this room, more than any other place, would trigger something. But nothing. It was like intruding into someone else's private space.

She had to start piecing together the last five years of her life. But where to start? Freya wasn't sure if she had a phone; she assumed she must, yet she hadn't been given it in the time she'd been in hospital.

'Mum, do you know where my phone is? Do I have one?'

Jillian grimaced. 'I believe it was crushed in the accident.'

Freya winced. She knew she was lucky to be alive but this detail about the accident made her shiver.

'Don't worry. Nico said he was going to get you a new one.'

That was kind of him. He must be a nice man; she had to trust that London Freya had had good taste.

'Cup of tea?'

The need for a hot drink was suddenly overwhelming. Freya followed her mother back down the stairs to the beautiful kitchen. It made sense the kitchen would be gorgeous; he was a chef after all.

Freya chose a chair at the table. Was this the chair she usually sat in? Or was it Niccolò's? Did they ever eat together? He was probably a good cook, but maybe he didn't like to cook at home. Did she cook? Had she finally learned to make more than cheese on toast?

Her eyes were drawn back to a green ceramic jug filled with large open blooms in pinks, yellow and reds. Gorgeous, but something she'd never had in her tiny apartment.

'Mum, what's Niccolò like?'

'What do you mean?'

'Exactly that. What's he like? You've met him. At this point you know him better than I do. I… I just don't remember him.'

Jillian reached for Freya's hand. 'He's lovely. He's been very good to you over the years. And he's very, very worried about you.'

That might explain the strained look permanently etched across his face.

'What did I tell you about him?'

Her mother laughed. 'All sorts of things. You've known him for years.'

Freya frowned.

'But we're close? I like him?'

'Yes, and yes. I can reassure you of that.'

Her mother couldn't answer all the questions she really wanted answers to: How were they when they were together? How did he feel about her? How did she feel about him?

Freya sighed. 'It's weird, suddenly living with a man I don't know.'

'But you *do* know him. You can trust yourself.'

Jillian placed a steaming mug in front of her. Earl Grey. Black. That hadn't changed. Freya clutched it like a lifeline.

'When did I move in with him?'

'Oh, a few years ago now. When he bought the place.'

They must have been good friends. More than just boss and employee.

Flatmates.

But was it anything else? Were they more than friends?

No.

Freya dismissed the thought again with a chuckle. Niccolò was a gorgeous, glamorous celebrity. But most of all, if she and Niccolò *were* an item her mother would have told her. Niccolò would have told her.

She wouldn't live in the attic; they would share a room. The list could go on. She nodded to herself, satisfied. They were friends, but not lovers.

Though how did London Freya manage to live and work so closely with a man like Niccolò and not be tempted...?

None of it made sense.

'How did I come to move in with him?'

'You were living in a dingy flat in South London and he suggested you move in with him to be closer to the restaurants. The office.'

It was his idea. Interesting.

'Can I please borrow your tablet?'

Her mother handed it over with a smile then moved about the kitchen, tidying up some things. Her mother looked more at home than Freya felt.

Google still existed, and still worked the same way. The homepage looked different, but that was hardly a surprise. She typed in his name, watching the predicted searches as she did.

Niccolò Rossetti.
Girlfriend.
Wife.
Shirtless.
Sexy.

The rest of the world was asking the same questions she was.

She'd move on to those searches once she'd figured out the basics. It wasn't dishonest, looking him up like this, was it? This was publicly available information, things that she should know if she was going to be living with the guy.

Stuff she had known. Once.

The basics were this: he was thirty-three years old, born in Puglia, Italy. That would explain his name and stunning Mediterranean looks. He moved to London when he was ten years old to live with an aunt.

Her throat tightened. What had happened to make him leave his home to live with a relative?

None of the reasons she could think of were happy ones and the website did not elaborate.

Niccolò started as an apprentice chef straight out of school and had worked his way around several restaurants in London and Paris. Some Freya had heard of but most she hadn't, though they sounded impressive.

The bio said he had opened his own restaurant about six years ago, in Islington. Freya didn't know a lot about the London restaurant scene but even she knew it was pretty impressive to open your own restaurant at twenty-seven. About four and half years ago he had landed a big book deal, and a television series followed. Since then, he'd written a book and produced a television series every year as well as opening two more restaurants. He was successful and getting more so. His style was everyday, practical food with an Italian bent. Fresh, healthy and easy.

His next anticipated project was a book and series titled *At My Mother's Table.* The mother he'd left behind in Italy.

She continued reading and watching videos as she drank her tea. Niccolò was seriously impressive. She'd been working closely with the sexiest celebrity chef in the world and didn't remember any of it. And Niccolò Rossetti did not have a face, or body, one forgot easily. A video of him kneading bread and smiling at the camera was still making her tingle fifteen minutes after watching it. It must have been some bump on the head to make her forget his brown eyes.

Freya glanced at her mother, who was cleaning up the kitchen with her back turned. She typed her own name into the search engine but then she gasped so hard her mother turned and exclaimed, 'What?'

Freya shook her head. She wasn't sure what she was expecting, but not this.

The search of her name brought up images of beautiful food, beautiful places. Some were instantly recognisable: a dining room with the Chrysler Building of New York in the background, another with the sparking lights of Paris. The photographs were bright, full of life and looked delicious. There were also links to interviews she'd given to all manner of people, including newspapers and magazines. The quotes attributed to her sounded like things out of another person's mouth, but most were about Niccolò: 'This is his best series yet… A fresh, modern take…'

As she scrolled down, the photos weren't just of the food, but of her. She was wearing clothes she didn't remember purchasing, standing in places she didn't remember visiting. Rome. Athens. Somewhere ice covered and Scandinavian looking. Her thoughts whirled. In some photos she was standing next to Niccolò. In others she stood next to strangers who looked glossy and fabulous.

It was a lot to get her head round.

In some photos she looked quite different. Her dark blonde hair, which was now straight and below her shoulders, was cut in a messy, textured, chin-length bob with highlights. A style she'd never been brave enough to try before. It suited her. She touched the screen with a single fingertip.

'Why didn't you tell me, Mum?'

'Tell you what?'

'That I'm famous.'

CHAPTER TWO

OKAY, SO SHE wasn't as famous as Niccolò Rossetti but she was quoted in goodness knows how many publications, and photographs she had taken were all over the web. As well as photographs of *her.*

Niccolò was really the famous one: as socially aware as he was talented, said one paper. Dark, sexy, looking as though he wanted to devour you through the camera, said another.

That he was called the sexiest celebrity chef in the world wasn't surprising, but that she worked for him was. Was she amnesic or simply hallucinating? If she did get her memory back, would she even believe it? What an amazing life she'd been living.

If I get back to work, back to my normal life, I might start to remember...

She sighed. Coming home to her house hadn't brought the memories flooding back; she was as confused as ever but now engulfed in disbelief.

'Are you sure this isn't a trick, Mum?'

Jillian laughed. 'Oh, love, no. Here—look.'

Her mother took out her own phone, scrolled through some photos and showed Freya a selfie she had taken right outside this very house. She was beaming.

'Now, go and lie down,' Jillian instructed. 'You've had a lot to take in and the doctor said to rest.'

Freya nodded. The morning had taken it out of her. She'd go upstairs, get into bed and maybe when she woke up things would be clearer. It was a faint hope, but it was all she had.

She walked into the hallway just as the front door was opening to reveal Niccolò coming in. He was wearing well-fitted black pants and a black sweater and coat. Mouth-watering. That's what they said about his food but it also described him perfectly.

'Hi,' he said. His lips lifted into a hesitant smile.

What on earth did he have to be nervous about?

'Hi. I'm going to lie down. Is that okay?'

He stepped towards her and she leaned slightly back. His eyes opened wide then quickly returned to their normal gorgeous size. 'Freya, of course it's okay. This is your house.'

'I know. It just feels like a stranger's.'

'It's not, this is *your* house. How are you feeling?'

She shook her head. She didn't even know where to begin. 'Overwhelmed. Confused.' But also, if she was honest, a little excited that she may soon recover the memories of the wonderful life she seemed to have been leading. And a lot nervous.

'Oh, I almost forgot.' He passed her a white box. 'It's a new phone. It should be all set up for you.'

She took the box and their fingers brushed. An electric shock pulsed through her but she flexed her fingers to shake it away.

'Thank you for getting me a new one. What do I owe you?'

Niccolò looked hurt. 'Nothing.'

'I can't just let you get me a phone.'

'Insurance. Insurance will cover everything.'

'But…' She began one question, then thought of another.

Jillian had shaken her head anytime Freya had asked about the accident and clearly didn't want to think about it, much less talk. All Freya knew was that she had been a passenger in a car and a truck hadn't given way.

'Do you know how the accident happened?' she asked.

He looked around the hallway as though choosing an escape route.

'Where was I? Where was I going?' she continued.

'I think we should sit down.' He motioned in the direction of the living room; a room Freya hadn't yet been into.

She followed him in and sat on the sofa, hoping at least the cushion remembered her shape, even if she didn't remember it. The sofa was as comfortable as it looked. Niccolò chose the armchair across from her, even though the sofa would have fitted them both with room to spare. He sat straight backed and rubbed the five-o'clock shadow covering his chin.

'We were going to lunch. For your birthday.'

'We?'

He looked ashen.

'You were with me?'

'I was taking you to lunch for your thirtieth birthday.'

'Oh, Niccolò, you were in the car as well? Are you alright?'

He gestured to his intact and upright form. 'Not a scratch.'

'I'm so sorry.'

'Why are you sorry?'

'Because…' She wasn't sure what she was sorry about but he looked as though his best friend had just died. 'Who was driving?'

'Ah, I was wondering when you would ask that.' He grimaced again and her heart dropped. Her memory might be a mess but this much was clear.

'It was you. You were driving,' she said.

'I'm the one who's sorry, so, so very sorry.'

'But it wasn't your fault—the doctors said the truck didn't give way.'

Niccolò nodded but the look on his face broke her heart.

* * *

It was all his fault. She needed to know the truth at some point and he had to be the one to tell her.

Freya sat on the sofa, perching at the front of the seat, like she was a guest in her own home, and it nearly broke him. How many ways was it possible for a heart to break? The sight of her looking nervous and perplexed in hospital was one thing, but on this couch? In *this* room? Why had he suggested they come in here? Anywhere but here. This sofa.

He couldn't meet her eyes. It was too much. Her confusion, her uncertainty, but most of all the fact that she looked at him as though he were a stranger.

'I should have told you,' he began. 'I'm sorry I didn't. I'm sorry—'

'No. I know it was an accident. I know you didn't hurt me on purpose.' Her eyes were wide and worried.

For an instant something like hope swelled up in him. She must trust him if she could be so sure that he wouldn't hurt her intentionally.

'The doctors said a truck was at fault.' she said.

His heart fell again. Technically, yes, but he knew that if he'd been paying better attention, he would have been able to avoid the lorry. But he hadn't and he didn't.

'Are you sure you're okay?' she repeated.

Physically, he was fine. He wasn't sure he'd ever

recover from the other scars. The last week had been like hell. Watching her being cut out of the car. Lifeless. Pale. Then watching her lie unconscious and unresponsive for days in the hospital.

Having to call her mother.

The joy at seeing her fluttering eyelids being shattered by the blank look in her eyes when she saw him.

'Freya,' he'd said, taking her hand. 'Thank goodness.'

'Who are you?' had been her groggy response as she'd snatched her hand away from him.

He'd had to leave the room to throw up. The guilt had been so paralysing he'd struggled for days to go into her room. Instead he'd hung around outside the room on the hard chairs, waiting for the doctors to give updates, for her mother to arrive.

Waiting.

Waiting.

But it was no more than he deserved.

She's home, sitting here, where she belongs. You should be grateful. It's all over.

Except it wasn't and never would be.

'Nico, darling, I thought I heard you come in.' Jillian appeared in the hallway. 'Can I get you something to drink? A cuppa? Something harder?'

'No thanks.' He moved to stand.

Jillian waved him down. 'You stay and talk. Tea?'

It had been both comforting and confusing to have Jillian here. Her presence reminded him of

Freya, of before, but Jillian wasn't Freya. And being reminded that Freya wasn't his Freya hurt even more.

But he acquiesced and remained seated. Freya moved slightly but assuredly farther away from him and his heart broke a little again.

His chest did not seem to stop aching. How much could one heart withstand? It was a question he'd had cause to ponder often over the past week.

'I'm the one who's sorry,' she said.

'You have nothing to be sorry for.'

'My mother's been staying here. You're being so patient with me.'

'This is your home.' How many times did he have to say it?

Until she understands. Until she remembers.

Freya looked slowly around the living room. After the kitchen, it was their favourite room in the house. It had a big, soft, comfy sofa and armchairs that were like sitting in a hug, a large television and an entire wall of books. She liked the view outside as well. The window was half a storey above street level, affording an easy view of the people walking past and the park across the road. Sometimes he'd catch her sitting where she was now, just watching the world go by.

Her eyes caught on one of the prints on the wall. It was a series of drawings of California. She'd chosen them. Would she remember those?

She's lost her memory. As far as she's con-

cerned it's five years ago, she lives in Pasadena and has a dead-end job with a horrible boss and a best friend who is about to betray her.

You? She doesn't even know you.

'I know…but…' she protested.

'What can I do to make you feel more comfortable?'

A pained look crossed her face. 'You can put up with me. At least until my memory is back.'

'There's nothing to put up with.' He tried to smile but smiles these days were in short supply. The muscles in his face tightened each time he tried to smile reassuringly.

She grimaced even more. 'You know there is. I told you everything in the hospital. I don't remember anything about my job, what I'm supposed to do. I don't know how to be a food stylist.'

'Is that what you're worried about?' Of all the concerns, that was the last thing she needed to be worried about.

'Of course. You're my boss and I just told you I can't do my job.'

'Freya, you've had an accident—that was my fault, by the way—and you have amnesia. I understand you don't remember some things.'

'I've forgotten everything.' Her voice was soft and instinctively he reached for her with his hand.

She recoiled and he regretted not exercising more control. He stood, went to the window but couldn't help pacing.

'Yes, I'm your boss, but I'm your friend first of all. I'm going to look after you.'

She screwed up her nose as though she didn't believe him.

'But I don't… I'm sorry, it's just so strange. You're famous, I'm nobody.'

He barked out a laugh. 'You're not nobody—please don't say that. We're good friends. Best friends.' Though those terms didn't even quite cover what she was to him.

'Best friends? You and I?' She laughed.

'What's so funny?'

'Because how? What do we even have in common?'

So much. We laugh at the same things. We share the same jokes. We like the same things and we don't care when we don't. We tell each other everything.

Maybe not everything.

How could he tell her what had happened between them? She had no idea who he was. That was apparent from the hospital. She'd thought he was a doctor, for crying out loud.

She wouldn't believe him if he told her *everything.* Or worse, she'd be even more upset and confused than she already was.

He had to wait for her to remember, in her own time.

Though doing that worried him just as much. Was he lying to her by not telling her?

Even if he was, he couldn't tell her what had happened between them the night before the accident. It would be far too confronting, given that she didn't even remember him. Yet he also hated lying to her. Every decision he made felt like the wrong one.

Jillian returned and put two cups of hot tea in front of them. 'I'm just going to finish packing,' she said as she left the room.

Freya looked longingly after her.

'You wish she wasn't going?'

She nodded and he got the feeling she was holding back tears.

You and me both, baby.

Freya shook her head and refocused. 'What do I do?'

'What do you mean? Now?'

'What do I do in my job? For you?'

Everything, he wanted to say. Instead, he swallowed the lump in his throat and said, 'You really don't need to worry about that now.'

'Why not? Are you going to sack me?'

'What? No! Freya, your job is open for as long as you need. I just want you to know that you don't have to worry about your work. You should concentrate on getting well.'

He didn't want her to quit. He couldn't lose her. She wasn't just his right-hand man; she was the whole right side of his body. He owed so much of his success to her. Professionally, personally. He didn't know where he'd be without her.

Yet after what had happened the night before the accident, could she stay working for him? Living with him?

'No, I have to know. It'll help me understand.' She waved her hands around the room. 'This. All this. And why I live here with you.'

He drew a deep breath and tried to be as honest and direct as he could. 'You're a photographer, food stylist and social media manager.'

She laughed. 'Is that all?'

It took him a beat to realise she was being sarcastic. He cleared his throat. 'I hired you as a photographer and the rest went from there.'

'That makes sense—photography was my thing.'

'At *The Southside Chronicle*.'

'You know about that?'

He nodded. I know all about you. I know your favourite colour is the same blue as the colour of the walls in the kitchen. I know your favourite place in the world is the beach at Leo Carrillo State Park and your favourite place in London is the rose garden in Regent's Park. Your favourite music is pop.

'You are going to be so excited to hear the new Taylor Swift albums,' he blurted without thinking.

'What?'

'Nothing, I'm sorry. You had—that is, you *have* a flair for designing food and know how to make it look amazing on film. You were a natural, and it went from there. I wasn't famous when I hired you. I was struggling with my first restaurant. You helped me become as successful as I am.'

She let out what sounded like a snort.

'You've been running my social media and publicity for years. We became successful together.'

'But I'm not—'

'Yes, you *are* successful. Look.' He took out his phone and pulled up a photo she'd seen earlier of her wearing an evening gown and holding a glass statue.

'That's you, getting a food photography award.'

She shook her head and buried her face in her hands.

'What else do you know about me?' she asked through her fingers.

'You love Taylor Swift.'

'Lots of people do.'

'She's released several albums in the past few years. We saw her at Wembley.'

'No way! That's awful!'

'No! You loved it. We had a great time.'

'It's awful because I don't remember. It may as well not have happened. No, in fact, it's worse than not happening because I'm jealous of myself.'

He stepped back towards her, wanted to hug her, and had to fight every instinct in his body not to.

'Your memory will return. The doctors are hopeful.'

You have to be strong for her. You know exactly

what it feels like, to wake up in a strange country and not know anyone around you.

It was terrifying when he'd first arrived in London. No English. His parents both dead.

'The doctors don't know. I think they expected it would've begun to return by now.'

His heart plummeted. He'd been hoping she wasn't worried yet. But clearly she was. The doctors began with plenty of optimism, but with every day that passed with no recollections, the less hopeful they became.

Freya had been diagnosed with traumatic retrograde amnesia. The physical brain injury she'd suffered in the accident had impaired her memory of events that had happened before the accident. However, the longer it went on, the more the doctors were worried she was suffering a type of dissociative amnesia, which may be due as much to psychological factors as to the physical injury. They were perplexed by the fact that it was specifically her memories from the past five years that were lost and not a random collection of events from her past.

This was Nico's greatest fear: that her condition had been triggered by what had happened in the days before the accident, rather than by the accident itself.

Freya did have memories. They had just stopped at a point that she had made a significant transition, when she'd been fired from her job at *The Southside Chronicle* and decided to move halfway around the world. And her memories recommenced when she'd woken up after the accident he'd caused. She had still been able to retain memories since regaining consciousness.

In other words, her brain had erased every memory of her life with him.

Which was fitting, since it had all been his fault. Nico had been subsisting on a couple of hours of sleep each night since the accident and was starting to get used to the sick feeling in his stomach. It was all he deserved.

Freya needed to rest, relax and not worry. And it was his job to see that she did.

'It's early days, and now you're home, things are bound to start coming back to you. I'm sure it won't be long.' He wished he believed what he was telling her.

She sipped her tea and pressed her lips together. Pink, full and soft as satin on his. He pushed the recollection deep down.

'What else do you know about me? What about us?'

He ignored the second question, the loaded, unanswerable one. 'I know that you're a ridiculously talented photographer, a lot of fun. Full of energy, ideas…' His tongue suddenly felt too big for his mouth and he paused.

She nodded. 'Then tell me about you.'

'Me?'

'I did look you up, but I want to know from you.'

'You looked me up?' *She's living with a stranger. Of course she looked you up.*

'Sorry, but I had to.'

'You don't need to be sorry. You should look up anything you want about me to make you feel more comfortable. But you can just ask me.' It was an invitation he wanted to withdraw as soon as he issued it. He could tell her many things, but not everything.

'Do you have a girlfriend?'

The tea churned in his stomach, empty apart from an apple he'd eaten six hours ago.

'No.' He said truthfully. *That* was what she most wanted to know? 'I don't. My last girlfriend was a few years ago and it wasn't particularly serious. I'm focused on my work and that doesn't leave much time for dating.'

She nodded, seemingly accepting his answer.

'Why did you move to Britain?' she asked.

'What did Professor Google tell you?'

'That you were born in Italy, but moved here when you were ten. But it didn't say why.'

He closed his eyes so he didn't have to look at her when he answered, 'I moved here to live with my aunt, my mother's sister. She brought me up after my parents died.'

'Of, Nico, I'm so sorry. I should've put two and two together.'

'No, it's alright.'

'They both died when you were ten?'

He opened his eyes but looked out the window instead of at her. It was easier that way. 'My father drowned in a boating accident when I was five. My mother passed away when I was ten.'

'Do you have any siblings?'

'No, but I'm close to my two cousins. I grew up with them. After.'

'That's lucky. I mean, none of it is lucky, but it's nice you're close to your cousins.'

He nodded and smiled. He knew what she meant. He'd always known what she meant.

'Was she good to you? Your aunt?'

'The best.'

His mouth tasted salty. His aunt, Cara, had arrived in Puglia shortly before his mother's passing and she and her husband had taken him in and raised him like one of their own children. However, there was no denying he was different. Dark hair, olive skin and a slight accent when he spoke English that he still hadn't quite shifted. Not that he wanted to. His Italian accent gave him an air of authenticity on British television that Freya called his Mediterranean edge.

Nico loved his adopted family fiercely, but that didn't mean he didn't miss his parents every day. He also wondered a lot about the place he'd left behind. While he'd returned to Italy for a few visits, he'd never made it back to Puglia and his home village.

'I'm sorry, I shouldn't pry.'

'No, please do. These are all things you know. You know me far better than Google.'

Freya frowned. 'I have so many questions.'

'And I want to answer them.' Just not *all* of them. 'I'm so glad you're home.'

His relief was physical. Yet as he saw her here, at this moment, sitting on the sofa, relief was tainted with guilt. He understood now why they called grief crushing; it weighed on him with each step and each movement, his body hurt, his limbs were heavy as concrete and his chest was tight. Sometimes it hurt even to breathe.

'Are you…? That is, has anything come back to you since you've been home?' he asked.

She yawned. 'No. Not yet.'

'Big day?'

'I was just on my way to have a lie-down.'

He jumped up. 'Go, don't let me stop you.'

She stood as well and lifted the hand that held the new phone. 'Thank you again.'

'Please, don't thank me.'

How could she be grateful when the fact that her old phone was pulverised was all his fault?

He shivered as she left the room.

They had been driving out to a new restaurant in Richmond for her birthday lunch when he'd failed to avoid the lorry coming onto the motorway. The police pressed charges against the truck driver but not against Nico. It might have been easier if they had.

There was nothing he could have done, the police had said.

Except they didn't know.

They didn't know that if he had been focusing properly, he probably could have avoided the lorry and the carnage afterwards. He should have avoided all of it. But he'd been weak. Done the very thing he'd vowed not to, and look where it had got him…

When Freya had finally woken up, three torturous days after the accident, he couldn't help thinking it was almost a blessing that she didn't remember anything.

He didn't want to stop her memory from returning—he wanted his best friend back more than anything—but he couldn't help thinking that it would be far easier on her if she didn't remember the day before the accident.

Because she would be far better off without him.

CHAPTER THREE

It was dark when Freya woke. A cup of tea was on her bedside table. She reached over and it was stone-cold. The clock at her bedside table flashed 10:00 p.m. The house was quiet.

She remembered the new phone Nico had gifted her and took it out of the box. Now if only she could remember her password… But the phone scanned her face and opened. She nearly dropped it. Heck, technology never stopped developing.

The good news was she recognised all the social media channels on her screen so started to look back over her posts. Much like the Google search, there were many photos of food and travel and people she didn't recognise but who she had tagged as friends. People who had tagged her.

She had friends. London friends. She scrolled through photos, partly curious, partly nervous. Nothing in her profile suggested she'd had any partners she didn't remember. And there were no photos of the same guy over and over. The creeping feeling came over her skin again. Something wasn't right. She hadn't had hundreds of boyfriends over the years, but had she really lived in London for five years and not found someone special? Even for a short while?

She wanted to remember things naturally, but on the other hand, not knowing how many other surprises awaited her was equally worrying.

She listened carefully for noise downstairs. Even though she didn't think Niccolò would enter her room without knocking, she didn't want anyone knowing about the search she was about to do.

'Niccolò Rossetti girlfriend.'

Nothing.

Well, not nothing. There was plenty of speculation. Photos of him standing with women at events. He even had his arm around some of them, but he wasn't kissing any of them. There were no pap shots of him holding hands with anyone. Then another thought occurred to her and she slapped her forehead. Of course.

She typed in, 'Niccolò Rossetti boyfriend.'

Again, there were heaps of hits. She scanned the results but no, despite many men obviously wanting it to be true, interviews confirmed that Niccolò was in fact straight.

Freya fell back onto her bed. In moments, she was asleep again.

It was morning when she woke. Dr Jamal had told her that having amnesia was exhausting. He had also told her that as hard as it might be, she should try to carry on with her life as normal.

After showering in her beautiful bathroom, she went to her wardrobe. She didn't recognise most of the clothes, but found a T-shirt she had bought at Leo Carrillo State Park. This was hers. She remembered buying it from a little place up from the beach. She must have brought it with her from home. It was a little looser than she remembered, but she didn't know if the weight loss was from after the accident, or earlier. How had she lost weight living with a celebrity chef? This new life really was too good to be true.

Freya walked carefully and quietly down the stairs, not sure if Niccolò was home and if she would have to go through another awkward encounter.

It shouldn't have been awkward, but it was. He was a stranger. A beautiful, gorgeous, sexy stranger who was trying to tell her that they were friends. Best friends. He'd really said *best* friends.

Her best friend was Jane. Yet no one had mentioned Jane.

Freya stopped on the landing of the second floor. She looked through the doorway of the room she knew was Niccolò's. The door was open, though not wide enough for her to see in. Still, the fact that it was left open indicated a degree of openness and trust that confused her.

She wasn't sure which part of the scenario with

Niccolò was weirder—that they were friends or that they were *only* friends. Hadn't London Freya wanted to sleep with him? How had she possibly managed not to?

Maybe he smelt bad?

No, she knew he smelt good. The whole house smelt good. Like clean carpet and expensive gift shops.

At that instant, Niccolò came through his bedroom door and she stepped back just in time to avoid a collision, but her face came within inches of bumping into him.

Caught!

The smell question was answered. He didn't smell bad; he smelt amazing, like clean and coffee and fresh croissants.

'Oh, sorry, I was just looking for Mum.'

'Please don't apologise. This is your house.'

Maybe it had been once, but didn't feel like it any longer.

'How are you feeling this morning?' He leaned forward, then leaned back just as quickly.

'I'm…' It was hard to explain, but was that because she couldn't remember the right words? 'Is there a word for "Okay, except that it feels like there is a big black hole in my head"? The Japanese probably have a word for it. Or the Germans.'

Niccolò grinned. He must think she was a fool.

'Physically fine. But tired,' she added.

He nodded. 'Jillian's in the kitchen.' He stepped back to indicate she should go first down the stairs.

Her mother was cutting up some fresh fruit and looked up happily when she entered, followed by Niccolò.

'Good morning! How are feeling?'

'Still no memory, if that's what you're asking.'

'Oh, sweetheart, it'll come.' She placed a bowl of freshly cut fruit on the table.

The three of them ate in silence. She looked from her mother to Niccolò and back again. This was ridiculous—these were the two people who allegedly knew her better than anyone in the world. She could ask them all the things she was worried about, couldn't she?

'Do I have a boyfriend?' she blurted.

'No,' Jillian said, shaking her head.

Relief flooded Freya's chest. She had deduced as much and it was good to have it confirmed.

'Have I had a boyfriend since Lachlan?'

Jillian and Niccolò exchanged a glance and panic rose again in her. She quickly waved her hands in the air as if that would erase the question.

'No, stop, no, don't tell me. I don't want to hear that I dated someone I don't know. I certainly don't want to hear that I've slept with someone I don't remember.'

She believed her memory would probably come

back in time but if there were any really bad surprises, she wanted to know sooner rather than later.

'What I'm asking, is, is there anything, anyone I should...? Oh, I don't know how to put it.'

Niccolò set down his fork and looked at her. Brown eyes turned down. Worried.

'What's the matter?' he asked gently.

'I know I need to let the memories come back naturally. The doctors have said that they most likely will. But what I'm worried about is why my last memories are in California. Why not London? Why don't I remember London? Did something happen to me in London that I somehow want to forget?'

Niccolò drew a deep breath and she noticed his body stiffen.

'As far as I know, and I've known you pretty well, the most traumatic thing that has happened to you in the past five years was the car accident.'

Freya exhaled, but Niccolò didn't look at all relieved.

'Nothing awful or traumatic or heartbreaking has happened to you that I know of,' Jillian added.

It was a relief to hear and that was all she needed at the moment. But there were still some things she wanted to know.

'Am I still friends with Jane?'

This time Niccolò and Jillian didn't exchange glances but both looked at the ceiling.

'Oh, my.' Freya's heart fell to her stomach. 'Is she okay? What happened?'

Jillian reached across the table for her hands. 'She's fine, she's well. She's still in Pasadena. Married. They're about to have their second baby.'

'Oh, that's great. Who is he?'

It took Jillian slightly longer than a beat to say, 'Lachlan.'

'Lachlan. Not…' But she could tell by the looks of pity on Jillian's and Niccolò's faces that the answer was yes. Jane, her supposed best friend, was now married to Freya's ex.

Niccolò stood and went to the counter to get a box of tissues. Freya stared at them but didn't feel like she was about to cry. She felt numb. Lachlan had dumped her a few weeks before her twenty-fifth birthday, telling Freya that he thought he should be with someone more 'high energy.' Freya had spent many waking moments since that point trying to figure out what he meant. She had plenty of energy.

Though her stupid boss at the stupid *Chronicle* had also implied as much.

You're not dynamic enough. Your work lacks vibrancy.

But Jane? *Her* Jane?

'How long? How? What?'

Even though she couldn't articulate the questions, Niccolò had the answers.

'It wasn't long after you got here. About the

time we met, actually. She was avoiding your calls and you thought it was because she was annoyed with you for leaving. Which she probably was. But then one of your other friends called you up and told you.'

Jane and Lachlan. Dating. Married. And they had kids together!

'You eventually managed to get her to answer your calls and she said how sorry she was, that she hadn't meant to fall for him, asked you to forgive her, blah, blah, blah.'

Freya might have giggled at his casual phrasing, if she hadn't been so shocked by what he was telling her.

'Did I? Forgive her?'

'You decided not to go to their wedding. They invited you, but you didn't go. We went to Paris for the weekend instead.'

We? She looked at him. Instead of going to her best friend's wedding—admittedly to a man Freya had dated for a year—she went with Niccolò to Paris.

Almost certainly a wise decision, but still a baffling one. To Amnesia Freya.

'You haven't really spoken to her since. You occasionally mention them but you're no longer hurting so much. You got over them once. I know you will again.'

It was the past for everyone else, but for her it was still the present. She expected to feel something physical, but she didn't feel anything. Like her body was already accustomed to it. Even though her brain couldn't even process it.

Lachlan and Jane? Jane had hooked up with Lachlan?

'Are you okay?' Jillian asked.

'I'm sure I'll remember in time, but please, please don't tell me anything else. Not yet.' This was enough to deal with for the moment.

Freya tried to eat some more breakfast, and Jillian and Niccolò pottered around the kitchen like they were old friends.

'The car's coming to get me in a few hours,' Jillian announced.

'I've told your mother that she can come back anytime she wants.'

'Or maybe you can both visit me again?' Jillian said.

'Again? We visited before?'

Niccolò and Jillian shared another conspiratorial glance.

'A couple of times. We spent a few weeks in California last year, filming a show. We spent a fair bit of time in Pasadena.'

'Right.' Freya crossed her arms. This was getting stranger and stranger. She thought maybe it was just London she'd blocked out, but it really was *all* of the last five years.

Everything to do with Niccolò.

'I'll pay for your flights,' he said to Jillian.

'That's too generous,' Freya said and Niccolò frowned.

They both had to get better at this. She had to start believing that he was her friend and that she could trust him. But he needed to realise she wasn't the Freya he knew.

She couldn't trust anyone at the moment, not her old friends and not even her own memory. The only person she did trust was about to get on a plane.

Niccolò turned to her mother and held his arms out. 'I need to get to the restaurant. Jillian, safe travels. Come back as soon as you can.'

'Thank you for everything.' Jillian stepped into his arms and they hugged.

It was like watching a movie. Her mother and this stranger were hugging, quite affectionately. Jillian patted his arm several times.

She had to try to start believing that this really was her life. Then maybe her memories would begin to come back.

Once Niccolò had left for work, Freya sat on her mother's bed and watched her pack. One of the only things in this house she recognised was her mother's suitcase. In a few hours Jillian would be gone and Freya would be truly alone.

'I don't know what I'm going to do without you.'

'You're going to be fine. I honestly think it's for the best. You need to get back to your real life and having me here probably isn't helping you do that. I wouldn't be getting on that plane if I didn't truly believe that you'll be fine.'

Freya sighed. 'What do you know about Niccolò?'

Jillian smiled. 'For starters, you call him Nico.'

Nico. That sounded too familiar for someone she hardly knew.

'I know you care a lot about him. I also know, without a doubt, that he really cares for you. Couldn't live without you. He's been beside himself. He didn't leave the hospital for a week. Has hardly worked since the accident. That's why he has to go in today.'

'But why? Why does he care so much?'

'You tell me.'

'I wish I could. I don't have any recollection of him at all. He doesn't even feel familiar.'

Jillian frowned. 'He's always been great to you. I've always wondered…'

Yes. Freya had been wondering the same thing.

'Why we're not together?'

Jillian nodded.

You and me both.

She definitely found him attractive. She had a pulse. And good vision. *Even if you were blind, you'd still be mad about him. His voice feels like the sun's caress on your bare skin. Each time he stands close to you his scent makes your head spin.*

'I guess because we're friends, we work together… Those are reasons, right?'

'Absolutely. Very good reasons.'

And maybe since they were friends, she'd seen his less attractive side. And maybe that dampened any attraction she might have felt? Maybe she'd grown to think of him as a brother?

'Take me with you.'

'Sweetheart.' Jillian walked over to the bed and held Freya's chin.

'This place is too strange.' Freya's cheeks began to wobble.

'The best thing for you, and you know it, is for me to go home. You need to do this on your own.'

'But…'

'You're so brave. I'm so proud of how intrepid you were to pack up and come here with nothing and build this life.' Jillian gestured around the room. 'Your memories will come back.'

Freya hung her head, knowing her mother was right.

She had to stay. If she never got her London memories back, there would always be five years of her life that were lost.

She also knew that you didn't get so many years in your life that you could afford to give up five of them. She'd recently come close to losing the rest of her years altogether.

The doctors and her mother had been cagey about the finer details of the accident, but Freya knew it had been bad. The fact her mother had travelled all the way from the States, as well as the anxious look on the faces of everyone she met, hinted as much.

Besides, while she had family in Pasadena, she had no job and apparently no friends either. Each time she thought about Jane and Lachlan she became a little angrier. Then a little sadder. Had they been planning it all along? Had Jane liked him from the start? Had London Freya understood all of this?

A car came for Jillian in the early afternoon. Her departure left Freya alone in the house for the first time. She took out her phone, the magical box that held so many clues to the past five years but none of the actual memories.

On a whim, she typed 'Jane Caruso' into the browser and the first things that came up were wedding photos. Freya winced at the bright smiles across both their faces and put down the phone. How had it happened? Why had it happened?

You weren't at the wedding. You went to Paris with Nico instead. She felt her thoughts begin to spiral but caught them. Niccolò was right; London Freya had moved on from Lachlan and Jane once before and she would do so again. She shut down the browser and opened her emails.

She scrolled through weeks of advertising but an email caught her eye. A plane ticket. Heathrow to LAX. One-way. She double-checked the day's date and then the one on the ticket. The ticket was for three days earlier. She was meant to be going to LA three days ago. She'd clearly missed the flight. Why had no one told her? With everything going on, they clearly had other things to worry about, but still. No one had mentioned it. Was she going to visit her mother? Grandfather?

Maybe they didn't know?

Impossible.

They would have told her about it. Someone would have mentioned it.

Why was it one-way? There was no return date.

Her head ached. The paracetamol package next to her bed was empty.

Freya went down a flight of stairs, head aching. She opened the first door on her right at the bottom of the stairs. Nico's. She walked to the en suite bathroom and opened the first cabinet on the left and there was the paracetamol.

She didn't linger long in the bathroom but instead stood in the bedroom.

The walls were a cool grey, matching the thick, soft carpet. But the rest of the room was coloured with bright accents. A large fireplace sat on one wall, lined on both sides with white bookcases, which in turn were filled with brightly coloured books and other objects.

A bright red armchair looked strange, yet was a feature of the room. She had an urge to curl up and sit in it with one of the books from the shelves.

You shouldn't be in here.

Freya left the room quickly, leaving the door slightly ajar as she'd found it.

It was only once she was in the kitchen filling a glass with water that she realised she'd known exactly where to look for the paracetamol.

This house was her home. She'd lived here for over two years. So what if she knew where the painkillers were kept? Chances are she'd helped herself to some before. Or fetched them for Nico. It didn't mean anything.

Except it did mean that her memory might be returning.

You found painkillers in a bathroom cabinet? That doesn't mean anything, everyone does that.

Except that she'd always kept hers in her bed-side table.

Freya groaned and rubbed her temples. So much for getting rid of her headache.

When she woke from yet another nap, the sun was low in the sky. She took an unfamiliar cardigan from her unfamiliar closest and wrapped it around herself. A delicious smell was coming from downstairs and she went to investigate.

Niccolò was sitting at the kitchen table with a laptop in front of him. He offered a broad welcoming smile when she walked in. Her stomach flipped. She smiled back.

'Hey, sleepyhead.'

'Hey yourself.'

His brown eyes sparkled. 'Hungry?'

'Starving.'

He served her a warm bowl full of an egg-and-tomato gratin, oozing with mozzarella cheese and with fresh bread on the side.

'This is amazing. Hands down the best thing that's happened to me all day,' she mumbled, mouth half full.

Colour rose in his cheeks. 'It's your favourite.'

'You made it?'

'Yes.'

'And I've eaten it a lot?'

He nodded very slowly.

He's afraid to tell me too much.

The realisation was sudden yet so obvious she wanted to slap her own forehead. He wasn't standoffish. He was just afraid of saying something wrong. Was he hiding something or just trying to protect her?

You can trust him, a voice whispered to her. *London Freya trusts him—you should too.*

'I don't know how I lost weight, living with you.'

He laughed. 'I think you may have lost a little since the accident, but don't worry, I'll make sure you get it back.'

Their eyes met and her body warmed. He cared for her. Deeply.

A memory of Lachlan telling her she should think about losing a few kilos came back to her.

Traitorous Lachlan.

Stupid Jane.

Those were memories that she'd rather stayed forgotten. The thought of actually finding out what had happened between Lachlan and Jane and the extent of their betrayal terrified her.

Freya looked away and took another generous mouthful of the comforting food.

London Freya had had five years to get past Lachlan and Jane. London Freya probably didn't think them about them very often at all.

She wanted to be London Freya. She wanted to become that person. The person who was Niccolò Rossetti's best friend.

But how?

'I want to go back to work.'

'There's no rush.'

'No, there is.'

'Yesterday you told me you didn't remember anything.' His eyes sparkled and her stomach flipped.

'I remember how to take a photo.'

He pulled a face.

Her face reddened. He was right; what business did she have waltzing to his office or studio or whatever it was and taking photos? She didn't know what her job involved. This was the worst type of imposter syndrome—because it was real.

'As your boss, I can't let you return until a doctor says.'

'Are you my boss, or my best friend?'

'I'm both. How about this? You have an appointment with Dr Jamal the day after tomorrow. Let's see what he says then. In the meantime, rest. I have to go into the restaurant tomorrow morning but I hope to be back by mid-afternoon.'

'Thank you, Niccolò.'

'Nico.'

'What?'

'Nico. You don't call me Niccolò—you call me Nico and I'd like it if you did again.'

Freya opened her mouth as if to repeat it but seemed to have forgotten how to say his nickname too.

'I'll be home mid-afternoon. I'll take you for walk around, see if that triggers any memories.'

'You're a chef. You run a restaurant. People eat at night.'

The thought was so obvious she couldn't believe it hadn't occurred to her before this. He laughed.

'We run three restaurants, but we have managers and talented head chefs in both. I can't possibly cook in three places at once as well as everything else.'

'We?'

'What?'

'You said "we" run two restaurants. Who is "we"?'

'I meant "we", the team.'

'Right, of course.'

His face reddened. He stood and went to the sink.

Nico returned home, as promised, just before two the next afternoon. He'd stayed in the office just long enough to check in on everyone and make sure they were managing.

Which they were. His team was at pains to push him out the door and go home to where they all said he needed to be.

To *whom* he needed to be with.

Everyone who worked for him knew how important Freya was to his business. They also knew how important she was to him. He was sure they all wondered why, given the closeness he and Freya shared, why they were not more than colleagues and friends.

The answer he gave when anyone asked outright was that they *were* colleagues and friends. What he and Freya had was far too important to risk.

She was on the sofa when he walked in, curled over her phone, looking confused. He noted the new crease that heartbreakingly hung between her eyebrows much of the time these days.

'Hey.' He stood in the doorway, waiting for her

to invite him to sit beside her. He hated, hated in his bones the pain he felt when she leaned away from him as though she was afraid.

Afraid of him!

She'd never been afraid of him. Maybe polite and cautious during their first few meetings, but after she'd been working for him for a few days and realised, quite naturally, what was missing from his business and what she could do for him, he felt that they had been equals. Still boss and employee, but she'd had no difficulties telling him what she thought he should do, and he'd had no problem following because when Freya had an idea about promoting his restaurant she was almost always right.

'Oh, hi. How was your day?' She sat up and smiled when she heard him.

He allowed a little relief to creep in and sat on the other sofa. 'It was good. Everything's ticking along. Lacey and Raff are managing to get along with one another, thank goodness, and Simon, I think, is loving having a bit more control in Chelsea.'

He saw the moment he lost her—at the mention of people she didn't know and problems that two weeks ago she'd been fretting over but now didn't know existed.

'What I mean is, the team is managing.'

She nodded. 'Anyway, I'm dying to go out and explore.'

'Are you sure you're up to it?'

'More than up to it. I'm going stir-crazy in here. I slept half the morning. I feel more awake than I have in days. I do still like to walk, don't I?'

He nodded and allowed himself a smile. 'Yes, very much. But if you get tired, we come back.'

He both longed for and feared spending time with her. He missed her desperately, but every moment they spent together brought new, painful reminders that she didn't know who he was. Freya wasn't the Freya he knew. The Freya he knew couldn't stop talking and loved to share things with him.

This Freya was more like the one he'd first met, recently arrived in London, shell-shocked and still recoiling from the betrayal of her friends. Still raw after being dismissed from her previous job.

She's still the same person. You just have to be gentle with her. She hasn't had the five years of healing your Freya had.

She came downstairs five minutes later wearing no more than a cardigan over her outfit, jeans and a blue T-shirt.

Even her style had changed since the accident. They were still her clothes, but she matched them differently somehow. He opened the hall closet and took out her navy blue coat. She eyed him suspiciously.

'Trust me. This is the coat you wear when rain is predicted.'

She took it slowly and he was careful not to let their fingers brush. That was not a sensation he needed to remember.

Outside he turned left as always but she turned right. They stopped, looked at one another. Her brow furrowed again.

'I'm doing it wrong again.'

He sighed. 'Not wrong. You usually walk this way. That way doesn't go anywhere. This way goes along the canals.'

'You know which way I walk?' Her tone was cautious.

'We often do this walk together. We can go that way, but if we go this way you might remember something.'

She fell into step with him and they rounded the corner. The canal came into view.

'I walk this way often?' she asked.

'Yes, but more often in summer. You do a loop, along the canal, to the park and—'

He stopped himself. He felt every bit of the burden in telling someone about themselves. It felt so wrong. Such an intrusion.

'It's okay, you can tell me. I want to know.'

'I don't want to put memories in your head.'

She stopped and smiled at him. For a moment he saw the trust in her eyes that had been there once before.

'I want to know. I need to know. Tell me everything.'

'Everything?'

'Tell me about us.'

'Us?' he scoffed and hated the way he sounded so dismissive. But what was he meant to say? *We were friends for a long time, but one day that changed. And then I nearly killed you.*

He couldn't tell her.

Not yet.

Maybe not ever.

Don't tell me, I need to remember myself.

'Yes, *us*. We work together, we live together, everyone tells me we're friends.'

He nodded.

'Then tell me about *us*. For starters, how did I come to work for you?'

This he could answer. 'I advertised for a food photographer and social media expert.'

'And I answered?' Her expression was incredulous.

He laughed. 'You did.'

She pressed her left palm to the side of her face. It was a gesture he knew meant she was thinking hard about something.

'Why on earth did you hire me? Were there no other applicants?'

'You're a great photographer. And you had journalism experience. Of course I hired you.' And she'd been honest, brutally honest about her lack of experience. And that had been the clincher. It wasn't often he came across people who were up-front. Unafraid to tell the truth. Freya always had. And he'd come to value that honesty, to rely on it. No, to depend on it.

She was the person who kept him grounded.

'But plenty of people know more about blogging and social media than I do. And I know nothing about food.'

He smiled at the memory. 'I asked you about that. I asked what experience you had with food.'

'And?'

'And you told me you loved eating.'

She winced.

'But that's the best qualification. A passion for food. I liked that you were so honest with me. I was starting out myself. I didn't know what I was doing. I'd opened my first restaurant six months earlier and it wasn't thriving. I'd been calculating how many more days I could afford to stay in business. But after hiring you, I didn't have to. Freya, I wasn't famous when we first met. It might help you to remember that.'

Freya had known more about food than she realised. She had a sophisticated palate and a real eye for colour and smell, but her feel for what made a good dining experience was innate. Her instinct for what was good and what was great had set her apart and had helped him grow his business. That had made her an integral part of his success.

And her enjoyment of food was positively seductive. He remembered the first time he'd cooked her his mother's seafood stew and she'd closed her eyes and opened her mouth in an almost orgasmic expression. Much like the look she'd given him when he'd fed her last night.

'But how?' she whispered.

'You learned about food. You learned how to promote a restaurant at the same time I did. We grew a successful business together.'

'Together?'

That was the wrong thing to say.

'We learned the business together. With your photos I landed a book deal. Then the television show.'

She scoffed. 'I'm sure it wasn't just my photos. I'm sure your innate sex appeal played a bit of a part.'

She gasped and her palm went firmly back to her mouth. Her cheeks turned the colour of tomatoes.

He laughed. Harder than he had in days. Harder than he had since before the accident.

'Sorry. I'm sorry. I know you're my boss, I just keep forgetting that. Along with everything else.'

Her boss. He was her boss. He sometimes had a certain amount of amnesia around that fact himself.

'They say I have a certain appeal.'

It was her turn to laugh. She mimicked him '"A certain appeal." I've read the reviews.'

'What else would you like to know?' he said but his tongue felt heavy. There were some things he wasn't ready to tell her.

We slept together and then I nearly killed you.

Some might say there was no cause and effect between the two things, but he knew the two things were connected. Because when he cared for someone, they died. It was what happened with his parents and it was what nearly happened with Freya.

'Why did I move in with you?'

'You were living down in Sutton.'

'Where even is that?'

'And you had weird flatmates who kept ferrets and stayed up partying all night. And it took you over an hour to commute. When I bought this place, I suggested you move in. It's closer. Much more convenient.'

He didn't add that she had helped him find this place when he'd got his second book advance and that he'd chosen it for the two of them to live in. Of course, they weren't together, just good friends. But he'd chosen the place because it was large enough for them to both share as friends, with each of them having their own floor.

'Can I ask you something else?'

'Of course.'

'It's a bit personal, but then I guess I live with you so I'd probably know. But it still feels strange to ask. Do you have a girlfriend?'

He smiled to himself. 'What did Google say?'

'Said no girlfriend. And no boyfriend.'

'Well, Google was right about that.'

'And when was…? Oh, don't worry.'

'Freya, you can ask me. You know me.'

'When was your last serious girlfriend?'

'Oh.'

He hadn't been expecting that question. Freya had known the answer to that and known that he'd been effectively single for the past five years. He'd had some casual flings, and had known she had too, but nothing serious.

'Um, four or five years ago.'

'Why?' she blurted.

It was a fair enough question.

'I've been busy. Running a multimillion-pound business isn't a piece of cake.'

She may not have intended to give so much away with her expression, but he knew it was her don't-mess-with-me-kiddo look.

'I've been busy. It's not easy to date when you're a chef—we work long hours.'

And some people just didn't want relationships. Some people just weren't made for them.

He was saved by the weather. The mist that had surrounded them developed into actual rain. He went to grab her hand, his instinct to pull her quickly in the right direction, but he remembered himself just in time.

'Come with me. I know somewhere warm.'

He led to her to the Red Crown, a pub where they had enjoyed countless casual evenings when he didn't want to cook and because she didn't.

They entered the warm room just as the rain was beginning to fall in earnest. Freya looked around and to his great relief headed in the direction of the table they preferred to sit at.

As though she remembered.

It's just a table. Anyone can see it's the best spot in the pub. It doesn't mean anything.

'Would you like a drink?'

'I think so. What's the worst thing that could happen—I might forget this evening?'

His heart fell.

'I was joking. Amnesia humour,' she said.

He should've been glad she found levity in the situation, but he wasn't.

Freya sat and he went to the bar and ordered red wines for both of them.

She looked appreciatively at the glass, picked it up and sniffed. 'Nice, thank you.'

He watched as she sipped slowly. Maybe the wine and being in a place she knew well would prompt a memory to surface.

'Can you please tell me about the accident?' she asked.

Nico pressed his lips together. 'You don't need to know about that.'

'I want to. I think I need to. But you and Mum have been so reluctant to tell me about it.'

There were good reasons for that. He could hardly bear to think about that day, let alone talk about it.

The car was on its roof. He couldn't remember it rolling, just like he couldn't remember climbing out of it, but he must have because he was standing on the road, barely a scratch on him, and she was still inside. He was frozen to a spot a few feet from the car. Too afraid to leave because she was in the car and he needed to be close to her, but even more afraid to step forward and see what was in the car. What was left.

Her hand hung, lifeless, from the smashed window, lying in the shattered glass.

He hardly registered the sirens above the noise of the traffic and the roaring in his ears but he saw the flashing lights, beating around him, making his eyes hurt.

'I was driving, I didn't see the lorry. I don't even remember the car rolling.'

'You have memory loss too?' Her eyes were wide.

I almost wish.

'There isn't much to say. The car was a wreck. It was a miracle I got out as I did.' That was all he could manage to say. He couldn't bring himself to think about that moment, let alone try to describe it. Why did she want to know about something that was so traumatic?

'It's not fair,' she sighed.

'I know. I'm so sorry.'

'I meant, it's not fair that you know more about me than I do.'

'You're right, that isn't fair.' A lock of wet hair had fallen across her face and without thinking he brushed it away.

Touching a hot stove would have been less painful.

She froze and he saw again the distance separating them. The way she looked at him like he was a puzzle. A stranger. Almost fearful. He was trying to make her comfortable, not to run.

'You'll have a break from me soon anyway. When I go to Italy.'

'Italy?'

He felt a stab in his chest. He hadn't told her.

Well, he had told her. They had planned the whole trip together. She'd spent the past year working on the plan with him, the places they would go, the dishes he might cook. She had even started writing the cookbook with him. This was the project they had collaborated most closely on, the one closest to his heart.

To both their hearts.

'I'm going to Puglia. Next week.'

'What for?'

'To research my next book and television series.'

'Why aren't I coming?'

'You were meant to, but I'm not sure you should

be leaving London at the moment. I need to go soon or I'll get too behind.'

'But I'm fine!'

He bit back a response. Physically she may be well, but they both knew she was not fine.

She sipped her drink and played with the stem on the glass as she always did when she was thoughtful. 'Did I have any other trips planned? Anything else booked?'

'No. Just Puglia.'

'Are you sure?'

'Positive.'

The look on her face made him uneasy.

'Then when do we leave?' she asked. The expression on her face was expectant, full of excitement.

'You're not coming.'

'Why not?'

'Because you're not well enough.'

'I'm fine. I feel fine.'

'Dr Jamal says you should stay in London until your memory returns.'

'No, technically he meant I shouldn't go back to California.'

There was nothing wrong with her ability to argue. The thought should have comforted him, but instead it was simply frustrating.

'I don't want to rush you, overwhelm you.'

'But if Dr Jamal says it's okay, I can go?'

He ran his hand over his head. 'I think you should rest.'

'You don't want me to go with you?' Her shoulders dropped limply.

'Of course I do. We planned this trip together.'

But now everything has changed. Now I know that the more time we spend together, the harder it will be for both of us.

This would be the first time he'd returned to Puglia since he'd been hurriedly packed off to live in the UK with an aunt. It was a trip he'd only had the courage to make with Freya's encouragement.

To go there without her would be heartbreaking, but to take her with him would be problematic. She had the best chance of getting better here in London. Every moment he spent with her reminded him of what he was going to have to give up. Every moment he spent with her made it harder.

He had to let her go.

He had to learn to live without her.

The thought of letting her go was terrifying. But the thought of something else terrible happening to her was even worse.

The following morning, Nico was in the kitchen, hunched over his laptop, going over the travel plans when Freya came downstairs. He sat up straight when she walked in the door.

'Can I make you something?' he asked.

She shook her head. 'I need to do it. I need to relearn where everything's kept. I tried to make a cup of tea yesterday and I didn't know where anything was.'

'If it puts your mind at ease, you don't use this kitchen much.'

'I don't?'

'You eat at the office. Or out. Coffee?' he asked, standing.

'Yes, please.'

He went about making her a cup of coffee using the machine she'd bought as she watched on. Standing a little close for his comfort.

'I really feel fine about going to Puglia,' she said. 'I feel as though I'm getting somewhere.'

'You can remember things?'

'No, not exactly, but…'

'What?' His heart jumped but he wasn't sure if it was from excitement or dread.

She sat at the table. 'It's hard to explain without sounding silly.'

He shook his head. 'Nothing sounds silly.'

'It's like you sometimes feel after waking up from a dream. I can feel some things. I know a particular emotion has flowed through my veins, but I don't know why. I can feel that something has happened—the memory is so close, just on the other side of a door. But I can't open that door.'

He nodded. 'It sounds so frustrating.'

'You don't know the half of it. The other thing

about amnesia is that you feel stupid. Most of the time. I know logically it isn't my fault. But I still feel silly. A lot of the time.'

'You don't have to come with me.' He put a macchiato down in front of her. Her favourite.

'I know. You've been so understanding, but I want to get back to work. And besides, I've never been to Italy. Oh, wait—have I?'

He laughed. 'No, you haven't. It was going to be your first trip.'

'Phew!'

'Why?'

'Because that's one less memory to have forgotten. Paris, New York, Amsterdam, Barcelona, all the places I've apparently visited in the past few years and I have no recollection of. So this will be great. I may not have all my memories but that doesn't mean I can't create new ones.'

It was difficult to argue with that logic. He longed to take her with him and yet what if she wasn't well enough? What if it disrupted her recovery?

'Please talk to Dr Jamal first.'

'Deal. But there's one more thing.'

'What?'

'Let me come with you to work today.'

Nico frowned. 'I'm not sure…'

'Just let me come with you. I'm going crazy just hanging around here. I just want to see where you work. Pretty please.' She made her fake pouty face and he was helpless to argue. He rubbed his temples instead.

'I won't do any work. I still don't understand what it is I do, but maybe coming in will help me remember.'

Again, it was difficult to argue. If coming home hadn't triggered any memories, maybe going to the restaurant would.

'Look at it this way—if you don't take me, I'll just try to find the place by myself. Are you really going to take the chance I'll get lost wandering around London alone?'

'No,' he sighed. He wasn't going to do that.

CHAPTER FOUR

FREYA WASN'T PREPARED for the number of faces that turned to look at her when she followed Nico into the restaurant. It was situated on a corner in what appeared to her to be a busy, slightly up-market part of London. The front door opened into a large light-filled dining room with high ceilings, white walls and subtle bright touches. The restaurant was three-quarters full, even mid-morning. The bustling kitchen was half exposed to the dining room but the entire space fell silent when she walked in.

She didn't usually have this effect on people.

A woman wearing a white shirt and black apron rushed over to her, arms wide.

'Freya! It's so great to see you!'

She enveloped Freya in a hug and Freya stiffened. *This woman's a friendly colleague*, she told herself, but then a man lined up to greet her and Freya pulled back. The faces surrounding her were lined with confusion.

'How are you?' another woman asked.

'I'm...' She looked to Nico. *Please explain to them.*

'She's fine, tired, but is still having some memory problems. She's come here to see if it helps her recall things, but please, go gently. I know it's strange, since Freya's such an important part of the restaurant and because we all love her so much, but please give her space and time. She'll come to you when she's ready.'

There were murmurings of 'Sorry' and 'So good to see you' as the crowd dispersed.

At some point in his speech, Nico had placed a warm hand on her shoulder, protecting her, keeping her close. Freya had to resist the strong urge to turn her head and bury her face in his chest. Coming here was more overwhelming than she'd thought it would be.

Because we all love her so much.

A woman appeared next and wordlessly handed her a mug of coffee with only a dash of milk. She sipped it and it was exactly as she liked it. How did the woman know?

Because she knows you.

The feeling of being unnerved rose up again in her. She focused properly on her surroundings for the first time.

'Wow, this place is beautiful.'

He laughed.

'What's funny?'

'You had several arguments with the decorators and builders to get it just right.'

'I designed it?'

'You did indeed.'

'Who am I?' she whispered under her breath. She caught him hiding a brief smile.

'Our office is upstairs. NRHQ.'

'Eww, who named it that? Let me guess, me too.'

He laughed. She loved his laugh, the way his face brightened, making that dark and anxious face burst into a smile that made her feel like the cleverest and funniest person in the world.

She followed him up a narrow staircase, also painted white like the rest of the space.

Freya stood in the doorway and surveyed the office. One desk was neat and orderly. There was a computer and a stack of tidily piled notebooks. A clean coffee mug sat just so next to the computer mouse. The desk against the other wall also had a computer on it, but that was the only similarity. It was chaotic, with stacks of higgledy-piggledy cookbooks. And no less than three dirty mugs. She had a feeling which was hers, but was afraid to choose. How much had she changed in the last five years?

'Do you know which desk is yours?' he asked.

'I want to say the messy one, but… I'm afraid I don't know who I am anymore and I may have turned into a neat freak.'

'No fear, the filthy one is yours.'

'Hey! You might have cleaned it while I was in a coma. Washed my mugs?'

A cloud fell over his face.

'I'm just kidding.' She picked up one of the mugs and sure enough a layer of grime was nurturing a healthy bacterial colony. 'I take it back. I am a reformed woman. I'll wash my coffee mugs out from now on in case I'm caught in intensive care again.'

The colour drained from Nico's face. No mean feat since his smooth olive skin was far from pale.

'I'm joking. Again.'

'It's too soon,' he said sternly and turned to his desk, though Freya noticed his computer wasn't on.

He's been a mess.

Her mother had hinted at how upset Nico had been.

If your best friend was in a bad car accident, you'd be upset too.

Freya stepped towards him and before she could think better of it reached out and placed her hand on his shoulder.

'I'm sorry that my attempts at humour have been a little black. I'm struggling with my stuff and I'm sorry for not thinking more about how this is affecting you.'

He didn't respond and he didn't turn to face her. She squeezed his shoulder gently.

When Nico turned, his eyes were glassy. There weren't tears in his eyes but there was definitely fog. He smiled and replied, 'If you're going to clean your desk, that must've been some bump on the head. When are you seeing Dr Jamal again?'

'Ha ha.'

She still held his shoulder and now he was facing her she realised how close they were. She held his shoulder like they were in a chaste dance. With one step, their bodies would be flush. He was about a foot taller than her and had to look down to her. She noticed his Adam's apple bob in a deep swallow.

Did they touch often? Were they touchy-feely friends? It was hard to believe they could be and that she'd have kept her hands off his glorious body for so many years. Studying his face close up, she saw the smooth lines, sharp corners and soft skin. Eyes you could fall into and lose yourself in forever.

She searched those eyes for hints and clues about him. About *them*. But it was almost impossible through the wall he now had back up. He'd locked the door to his thoughts and he wasn't letting her in.

Nico looked away and the chance to discover more about him was gone.

'I have to get down there. Settle back in and hopefully…' He didn't need to finish that sentence. They both understood what he'd left unsaid.

The office was both bright and cosy. It looked out onto a small park and afforded a view of the sky. The walls were covered in maps and posters of food. They shared an office. And a house. Didn't they get sick of one another?

She picked up a cookbook that was sitting on her desk. She opened the hard, glossy cover.

Winter Warmth
By Niccolò Rossetti and Freya McFadden.
Photographs by Freya McFadden.

Wow.

She wasn't just a published photographer but an author too.

She flipped the pages. The book was full of beautiful photographs of food that were making her mouth water. Finished dishes of warm stews and curries, bright, healthy ingredients. Photographs of the cooking process. Tables laid out beautifully. She recognised some of the shots were taken in the restaurant downstairs.

You took these.

Freya sat at her desk for a while with her hand on the book, breathing deeply. She had done this. It was so far away from *The Southside Chronicle*, Jane and Lachlan and her life in Pasadena.

I need someone with more energy. You aren't dynamic enough.

What did they even mean by saying those

things? Had Lachlan always preferred Jane? Had Jane always had a thing for Lachlan? Was it Jane who encouraged Freya to leave the country? Get her out of the way?

You sure did show them all.

She wondered if London Freya had posted a copy of this book to her old boss with a note inside saying, 'Vibrant enough for you?'

Probably not.

Had London Freya sent a copy to Lachlan and Jane with a note saying, 'I don't need either of you!'?

She doubted it.

London Freya probably didn't give Lachlan or Jane or anyone at *The Southside Chronicle* a second thought these days. Yet for Amnesia Freya the hurt was still fresh. The events still confusing. Jane? Her best friend, Jane? That betrayal was far worse than being sacked or Lachlan dumping her. This was Jane. Nico had been wrong; she *had* suffered a heartbreak since coming to London.

You could call her. Ask her why.

Freya stared at her phone. She hadn't spoken to Jane in years, apparently. They no longer had a relationship. And once Freya began to get her memories back, she'd also remember how she managed to put Jane and Lachlan out of her thoughts and move on.

She opened the heavy cookbook still on her lap. Niccolò's introduction spoke about the importance of food in the colder months for physical and mental health. He wrote about traditional winter feasts and celebrations. It was nice, inspiring stuff.

Then she read what she had written.

> It's no secret that those of us from SoCal tend to struggle with London winters and I was no different.
>
> These are the dishes that Nico cooked for me that first, cold, wet and lonely winter when I was struggling to make my way in my new home. These dishes will comfort you too. Some will give you strength, others solace. I hope they bring you the same joy they brought me.

How was she not *with* this man? The Freya who wrote that introduction sounded like she was utterly in love with him.

The computer on her desk was an unfamiliar model, but she found the on switch and managed to boot it up successfully. But what were the chances she'd use the same password?

Very high, as it turned out. It was still her old street name and the last digits of her mother's phone number.

Hundreds of emails popped up, from names she didn't recognise, with subject headings that made no sense. Proof. Drafts. Scripts. Finals. Italy. Puglia. Puglia. Puglia.

Her thoughts spun and it took a while to focus on one message at a time.

The emails were mostly business related, about the Italy trip, the cookbook and series they were working on. She would get to those when she had more of a handle on things. An email from Nico caught her eye and she opened it.

The itinerary looks fab, don't know what I'd do without you xx

Now, granted, the last boss she could remember had sacked her because her photographs were not eye-catching enough, but bosses didn't usually sign off emails with kisses, did they? Maybe this was another five-years-in-the-future thing?

She took out her phone. It was logged into her account. All her messages were still there.

She'd deliberately not looked at them before this, afraid of what she might see. Afraid of what she might assume or interpolate. Afraid they would just confuse her further.

Could she get more confused than she already was? No, she couldn't, she decided.

Nico Rossetti was at the top of her message list.

She closed her eyes, swallowed and clicked. There were hundreds. No, probably thousands of messages between them.

Some were administrative: Where are you? What time are we leaving? What's the address again?

And some nonsense messages that made no sense to her, but indicated a deep, close relationship between them.

Others were links to all sorts of things: newspaper articles, videos. There were memes, photographs.

Photos!

She opened that app.

There was a lot of food. But also places. It was like looking at the photos she'd seen online, only a million times more so. She didn't recognise any of the faces in the photos, except for Nico.

She scrolled and scrolled and lost track of time. So much for her vow to let her memories come back in their own time.

A photo of Nico appeared on the screen. He was standing in a kitchen, smiling at the photographer. Her. He'd been smiling at her. His entire face was lit up, his brown eyes focused entirely on her.

This photo.

She could fall asleep looking at that photo.

But had she?

He's always been great to you. I've always wondered why you two aren't together.

She'd been wondering the same thing. The more she got to know him the more she liked him. She was attracted to him, had been from the start. Surely London Freya must have been too. And if thirty-year-old Freya was falling for him as a stranger, wouldn't twenty-five-year-old Freya have as well?

We work together. We're friends. It seemed like a plausible explanation to Freya. It was what everyone else believed, but did she?

Her gaze fell back to the email with the airline ticket to LA. One-way. Nico didn't know about it; that was clear from their conversation last night. Was she leaving London without telling him? Why on earth would she do that? What was London Freya running from?

One week later, and after checking with Dr Jamal, Freya's carefully designed itinerary had landed them both in Bari, the largest city in Puglia, on the sparkling Adriatic coast. They'd picked their hire car up from the airport and driven into the city and to their hotel. He had asked her to drive, claiming that she was more accustomed to driving on the right than he was. That was true, but it wasn't the real reason. The real reason was that he wasn't about to get behind the wheel of a car with Freya sitting next to him ever again.

The plan was to spend a night in Bari before driving down the coast to Monopoli, the town they would base themselves in. From there it was a short drive to Tregua, the village where he'd lived the first ten years of his life.

Freya pulled up at the hotel and he looked over to her, blinking in the sunlight. She was looking a little washed-out after their trip but her eyes were wide with wonder, taking in the bustling street and the seafront across the road, filled with pedestrians enjoying an evening stroll.

The itinerary they had planned was mostly eating, drinking, visiting local markets. Talking to some chefs. It had been designed to be an amazing trip for both of them. Just the pair of them, drinking, eating, enjoying the sunshine.

Things they had done many times in the past. But that had been *before*.

Before the night they had shared.

Memories were a funny thing. Freya wanted hers back but he was being tortured by his own. By the thought of her lips, her hands on his face, the smell of her body, the way desire had rolled through his.

Every single one of his muscles tensed. He swallowed, regrouped and turned back to her.

'How about we freshen up before dinner?'

A cold shower and a change of clothes would fix everything and he'd be able to think straight again.

The effect of the cold shower and clean clothes lasted approximately five minutes, until Freya arrived in the hotel lobby wearing a green cotton dress with thin straps. The beautiful skin of her neck and shoulders was bare and luscious and he had to swallow hard and bite back the memories of the night before the accident.

He couldn't remember her wearing this dress before. He'd noticed that lately her style had changed. While she was still wearing items from her wardrobe, she wasn't wearing her favourites.

She must've caught him looking at her because she rubbed her arms and said, 'I know, I know. I'm so pale. Did I get any sun in London?'

'You stopped missing Californian winters eventually.'

'I did?'

He nodded. 'After three or four years.'

She winced.

'I'm sure you'll get your dose of vitamin D here over the next week.'

Nico led the way through the cobbled streets of the old town to the bar she'd chosen for them to try. Sounds of conversation and laughter floated out into the street as they passed open doorways. The bar was tucked away in a narrow alley and looked inauspicious until the aromas hit his nose. They ordered a selection of drinks and dishes, including curled octopus, calamari, king prawns. Bari was famous for its seafood.

'I thought this was just predinner drinks?'

He laughed. 'It is. We won't eat everything. We'll just try things. For research purposes.'

Her bright blue eyes were wide. 'How are we both in such good shape?'

He laughed again. 'We walk a lot.'

Conscious he was using the word *we* a lot, he pulled his notebook out and started taking some notes.

'Research?'

'Always.'

'What are you writing down?'

'Everything. The setting, the set-up, the menu.'

A selection of shareable dishes arrived and he couldn't help but salivate. Though at least it was a change from salivating over the gorgeous woman across the table from him.

She drank her ruby spritzer slowly and swirled it contemplatively.

'I imagine you already told me all about it, but could you humour a poor gal with amnesia and tell me again? What happened to your parents?'

He nodded, buying time while he decided if he would tell her the long version or the short version.

This is Freya. She knows the long version, so you may as well tell her.

It wasn't a story he brought to the surface of his consciousness often. Hardly ever.

'I was five when my father died, ten when my mother passed.'

'What happened?'

He took a deep breath. 'My father drowned. He was fishing and the boat capsized. I saw it from the dock. I screamed for help but they couldn't make it in time.'

'You saw it?'

He nodded.

'And you were five?'

He nodded again and she exhaled a profanity.

The look on Freya's face was almost identical to the one she'd given him nearly five years ago when he'd first told her the story. As though she could physically feel his pain.

'Oh, Nico, I'm so sorry.'

'There was unexpected wind and the boat capsized. I called for help, but not fast enough. I remember just standing there, watching, being unable to move and…' It didn't do to dwell on that feeling, panicked, unable to run or scream. Feeling like his feet were stuck in concrete. 'It was a bit like a nightmare.'

'Only real.'

He nodded. 'Mama was devastated. They loved one another so much. She left her life in England to live with him here. Her family wasn't overjoyed by the idea of her giving up everything for a poor Puglian fisherman. But they ran a restaurant together, they had me and…'

'And they were happy.' It wasn't a question. She knew.

'So happy. And when he was gone, she died of a broken heart almost five years later.'

'Not really?'

'Yes. That's what they said.'

'Is it really a thing?'

'Yes, it is.'

'I believe you.'

She reached over and took his hand. A gesture his Freya had done many times before, but it was the first time for *this* Freya.

What he didn't say, what his Freya had known, but what this one did not, was how it was all his fault. He wasn't foolish enough to think that he'd caused the boat to sink, but he hadn't been able to get help fast enough. He had just watched it happen.

And she also knew that after his father had died, Nico's own love hadn't been enough to keep his mother alive. She had died of sadness. Her grief had killed her.

He could not protect the people he loved. The day after he'd let his guard down with Freya was the day before he'd almost killed her. This was why he didn't let anyone too close to him. His work and ambition were a convenient and believable excuse, but the real reason was far more important: how could he let anyone love him when he knew he couldn't keep them safe?

After sampling the dishes at the bar, they

walked to their next destination, a restaurant overlooking the port.

They were taken over to the best table in the place, with a view of the water and the boats bobbing up and down. They were treated to a spread of various dishes, orecchiette with broccoli, tuna tartare, smoked burrata and a Puglian speciality, *spaghetti all'assassina*. Or burnt spaghetti.

'Not actually burnt?' Freya asked.

'The fresh pasta isn't boiled, but cooked directly in the pan, in a sauce and then a broth.'

Freya knew this. He'd cooked the dish for her several times and she'd loved it. She couldn't wait to sample it on this trip.

But that was before the accident.

'Do I like it?'

He swallowed, though it wasn't the wine moving down his throat but fear. It scratched and burned all the way to his gut.

It was her memory. She'd forgotten what it was like to be herself and he mourned for her and himself all over again.

Such a stupid little thing, the dress she was wearing, her favourite drink, her favourite food. It shouldn't mean anything but it did. Because it shocked him again just how much was missing, how much might be lost forever.

Suddenly the weight of what was ahead for both of them in the coming weeks or months was too terrifying to contemplate. Fortunately, Freya was oblivious to the fear washing through him. She looked around the restaurant and sighed.

'Is this what it's usually like?'

'What? We've never been here.'

'No, I mean, travel, food. Us.'

Us.

His thoughts snagged on that word.

Was there even still an *us*? Would there ever be again? If she regained her memory, she'd want to leave anyway. Just as she had before. Leave London. Leave him. And this time he wouldn't be able to stop her.

'Pretty much.'

'We're so lucky. Is it possible to be jealous of yourself?'

'Your memories will come back.' He was reassuring her as much as himself.

He wanted her back—his Freya—yet at the same time was terrified about what that would mean when it did happen. Would she remember everything? Even the day before the accident?

Was it horrible for him to want her *not* to remember that?

Yes. He was horrible. It was all his fault.

Everything that happened was his fault and one way or another he'd have to live with it.

'Was I happy?' she asked, looking into her dish.

'I think so.'

Except at the end. At the end he wasn't making her happy. He was unsure how long she'd felt that way, but it had been long enough.

'You think so?'

'I mean, yes, you were. For most of the time at least.'

Her brow creased. 'Did it take me a long time to get over Lachlan and Jane being together?'

'Oh. I see. You were a little angry at first, but no. I don't think it took you all that long.'

She pulled a face. She'd been outraged when she'd first found out about Jane and Lachlan. If she could forget both of them and their betrayal for good, that wouldn't be a bad thing.

'Then what did you mean when you said, "For most of the time at least"? Was there something else that went wrong?'

'No, nothing like that. Your mother and I told you.'

'Then what?'

'I think...' He made a show of twirling his pasta but he was really choosing his words very carefully. 'I think as your thirtieth birthday approached you were thinking a bit about the future. About your next steps.'

'I was? Wasn't I happy working for you?'

'Freya, it's been a long time since I said you worked for me. I always say you work with me.'

She let out an incredulous laugh.

'It's true. You have to believe it. So much happened over the past five years, to you. To both of us.'

She sat with this thought for a while and looked out over the water. The sparkling Adriatic had darkened as they'd been eating.

'What on earth could I possibly want to do apart from this?' She waved her arms around the beautiful setting they found themselves in.

He shook his head. 'I honestly don't know. I didn't want you to leave.'

Oh. He'd said too much. But he didn't want to lie. It was impossible.

She put down her fork. 'I was going to leave?'

This conversation was tying his gut in as many knots as the spaghetti on his plate.

'I don't know. I hoped not. It was just something you mentioned the night before the accident. What your thirties might bring.'

'Oh.'

She nodded as though she understood. He hadn't lied. Not exactly. There was a fine line between answering her questions honestly and replacing her memories.

He watched her eat and think. She twirled her shoulder-length blonde hair absent-mindedly around her index finger, creating tiny curls. He rubbed his own fingertips together, remembering the silky sensation of her soft hair in his hands. Her blue eyes wandered over the bustling restaurant and then to the relative calm of the sea. Her eyes were still beautiful, still thoughtful and intelligent, but now were missing some of their familiar spark.

She's a lot like the Freya you first met. Young, uncertain. Hurting.

Yet she'd always been more than that. Also full of fire and passion, energy and enthusiasm.

She's still your Freya.

His heart sank.

She'd never be *his* Freya. And he had to stop letting himself think otherwise.

'The memories will come back. Probably when I least expect it,' she said.

And that was one thing he was afraid of.

CHAPTER FIVE

FREYA OPENED THE shutters of her hotel room wide and had to shield her eyes from the bright morning sun. The heat and sun reminded her more of California than London. The change of scenery was good for her, no matter what Nico might think.

She felt better in the Mediterranean sun. Her memory might not have returned but the air and the light here were invigorating. And that had to be a good thing.

Dr Jamal had assured them both that a trip away should be fine and not disrupt her recovery too much. He'd also assured her that if she felt well enough to drive then she could. Nico had been reluctant for her to come, but he couldn't argue with the doctor, who was adamant that if Freya felt well enough to go, then she should. Getting back to work, getting back to normal, was the best thing she could do now.

The doctor's unspoken words were, *I expected your memory would have returned before this.*

You'd better just accept the situation and start adjusting.

So adjust she would.

And if her memories never came back, well then, she'd just have to make new ones.

As apprehensive as she was to recover her memories, the thought of never getting her memories back at all was more worrying. But only just. Why had her brain only blocked out the years she had been in London? The years she had known Nico. Dr Jamal had again brought up the possibility that she was suffering from dissociative traumatic amnesia due to a psychological event, rather than the physical one, so the fear that something awful had happened to her while in London lingered at the back of her mind. Nico was the last person she could tell about those fears, especially since she had insisted so vehemently that she was fine to come with him to Italy. She had bluffed her way onto this trip, but she had no idea what her role actually was. What was she meant to be doing? Nico was taking notes. She was just eating and drinking, which was fine as far as it went, but it didn't seem like work.

You should be taking photographs.

She'd packed her camera, her London camera, but hadn't actually taken it out of its case since she'd returned from the hospital. She hadn't even taken any photographs with her phone.

Your work lacks vibrancy.

You aren't dynamic enough.

I need someone with more energy.

London Freya must have pushed those voices aside and got on with her life.

Why couldn't she have forgotten her stupid old boss and her awful ex and their cryptic insults and remembered all the adventures she'd had with Nico? Stupid memory. Stupid amnesia.

She showered and went about the task of choosing an outfit. It was lovely having London Freya's wardrobe to choose from, though it felt a little as though she was playing dress-up. She chose a calf-length navy blue linen dress that California Freya would never have picked for herself, but which she had to admit looked very sophisticated on her. She paired it with some white sandals and hoped it would be suitable for whatever the day held.

Nico was already waiting in the lobby when she came down. She caught a smile quickly pass over his lips before he suppressed it by pressing his gorgeous lips tight together. As if to suffocate the smile.

Instead of pondering the significance or otherwise of his expression, she pressed on.

'Where are we going for breakfast?'

'A place just down the street,' he answered.

'Is it good?'

'You've always wanted to go there. You struck up an online friendship with the chef.'

'Oh.'

She had had just as much of a hand in organising this trip as he had. And going to this restaurant was probably something that two best friends would have enjoyed doing, less so something Nico felt like doing with Amnesia Freya.

'I'm sorry,' she said.

'What for?'

'You and Freya planned this trip together and you get stuck going on it with me.'

'Newsflash, you are Freya.'

She sighed, 'But I'm not your Freya.' She stepped out onto the busy morning street.

Nico grabbed her hand and pulled her back. 'You will always be my Freya, no matter what.'

She managed a weak smile.

He held onto her hand as though he was used to holding it. As though it was something they did.

She wanted to lean into him. Smell him, taste him.

His scent was familiar somehow. Was she remembering it from before, or just from the last week? He smelt of laughter, lightness and…longing.

How had London Freya withstood it? Being next to this gorgeous man day after day? Or had she felt nothing for him? The more time they spent together, the closer she felt to him. The more she was drawn to him and the harder it was for her to step back and away. He drew her to him like a sun.

What had London Freya thought of him? What had she felt for him? How could she have been immune to his olive skin and kind eyes? Or those full lips that quirked ever so slightly in one corner when he looked at her? How had she possibly kept her lips away from his?

Nico led the way through a bustling market, filled with colourful fresh produce and the smell of freshly baked bread and down a lane lined with overflowing shops. The city was beautiful, full of so much colour and life, but it was hardly registering when all she could think about was what on earth had been going on between her and Nico.

He stopped outside an unassuming cafe. Before either of them said anything a man emerged from behind the counter.

'*Ciao*, Niccolò!'

The men shook hands and then he turned to Freya.

'*Bella* Freya!'

She smiled, nodded and wasn't prepared for the hug he pulled her into.

'How are you feeling?'

She shrugged. 'Okay.' It was the only possible response.

'Freya, this is Gino. The owner of the cafe,' Nico said, before speaking in Italian to the man. Freya assumed he was letting Gino know that she hadn't regained her memory because Gino then tilted his head in the universal sign for sympathy.

'Never mind, you will still enjoy your meal!' Gino said happily in English.

Gino brought them coffees and a selection of pastries with every conceivable filling.

She eyed the spread in front of them. 'Is this our only breakfast or should I leave room for a second breakfast?'

'We're going to have a walk around one of the markets, but eating is optional. And then we're driving down the coast.'

'To your village.' She remembered this from the itinerary he'd shown her. Tregua was the village he'd grown up in, to which he hadn't returned since he was ten. After his parents had died. She didn't know why he hadn't visited since his father's family still lived there and he had travelled to Italy. She wondered if it was because of the way his father had died. Freya shivered at the thought of how powerless he must have felt watching his father drown.

Freya had been there when her father had passed away, but he had gone slowly, of cancer. They all got to say their goodbyes and there was nothing left undone or unsaid. And that was still awful. But to be five years old and to blame yourself? She wanted to reach for Nico, pull him to her.

Though that was an equally confusing thought.

'Yes, and then Monopoli.'

'Why aren't we staying in the village?'

'It's very small, there isn't a hotel or anything and I don't want to intrude on my aunt. She's nearly eighty. She's my father's aunt, so my great-aunt. Anna.'

Freya nodded.

'How do you feel about going back? Excited? Or nervous?'

He smiled. 'Honestly? I'm not sure. I am excited but I've been thinking a lot about the past lately. And that isn't all pleasant. Sorry, I shouldn't be telling you all this.'

'Why on earth not? You told London Freya.'

'London Freya?'

'That's what I've been calling my other self.'

He screwed up his face as though he didn't like what she was saying.

'You can tell me what you're thinking and feeling. I know the past few weeks have been all about me and my health, but you're allowed to have feelings too. You can talk to me. I don't need my memories back to understand that this will be a difficult time for you. I think I would feel excited and curious but also apprehensive and sad.'

Nico stared at her, his brown eyes wide and his jaw slack. She slipped her hand into his and squeezed. It was warm and strong and she wanted to keep her hand in his forever. She felt his hand tighten around hers for the briefest of glorious moments then he let go, closed his eyes and drew a deep breath.

'Yes, I feel all those things. I've been thinking about my parents a lot since we've been here.

'That's understandable.'

'And missing them more than I have in ages.'

'That's also understandable. They'd be so proud of you.'

Nico looked down and she heard him sniff back emotion. Then he shook his head. 'You don't know that.'

His sadness hit her in the chest. 'I do. I may not remember you, I may not know you like London Freya does, but I still know that you're a wonderful person, that you have done some amazing things. Including how you've been looking after me.'

Her mouth went dry when she said those last words. She was parched and she looked around for some water. There was none on the table so she turned to catch Gino's eye.

She didn't spot Gino, but she did spot her own reflection in the mirror behind the counter. She caught Nico's reflection too. He was looking up again, leaning forward.

Looking at her.

His mouth hung open slightly, his head tilted just a little, and the look in his eyes was unguarded. Dreamy.

He's looking at you.

Her stomach flipped and she had to look away, feeling like she'd seen too much. Intruded on something that wasn't for her. She blinked and Gino appeared next to her, bringing a bottle of water as though he'd read her mind.

When she turned back to Nico, he was studying his coffee and his face was once again blank.

They left the cafe and strolled along the cobbled street to the busy market, fully in the swing of the mid-morning bustle. People of all ages were buying their fresh bread, meat and vegetables. The sounds and the smells were something to behold.

But the colours!

Without thinking twice, she took out her phone and took some snaps of the fresh fruit, lined up in neat boxes of colour. The flowers of every hue, the breads and the vast array of seafood.

She noticed Nico, watching her, rubbing the day-old growth on his chin.

Oh, to do the same. To run her fingertips across that gorgeous stubble. To press her lips to it. Rub them along it.

She bit back a huff of frustration.

It didn't make any sense: she was attracted to Nico. Pure and simple. There were so many things she didn't know at the moment, but that was one fact that she knew without a doubt.

So wouldn't London Freya also have been attracted to him? Unless the bump on her head had triggered new feelings in her. Could amnesia do that?

She wanted to call Dr Jamal but how could she ask such a thing? Could amnesia make you lust after your best friend who you've had a completely platonic relationship with for nearly five years? Could a bump to your head change someone's desires so completely? Maybe a head injury could make you see the world in a different light. Maybe trauma could also make you realise how short and fragile life was and compel you to make the most of it.

She took some more photos of the market and looked on while Nico chatted to the stall owners in Italian.

Maybe London Freya was attracted to Nico but knew he wasn't attracted to her. Even as she asked herself the question, answers started popping into her mind. The look he'd given her when she'd walked into the hotel lobby last night in the green dress. The way he'd reached for her hand when she'd stepped onto the busy road.

The way his eyes widened when their faces were close.

The way he was looking at her in the cafe when he thought she couldn't see. Were they the actions of a worried, caring friend or something else? Something more intimate?

But maybe she was going about this all wrong. Maybe it simply didn't matter how London Freya felt about Niccolò. What mattered was how this Freya now, Amnesia Freya, felt about him.

She was hopelessly, crazily attracted to him. She had to make a conscious effort not to touch him when he was near. Not to lay a palm on his strong bare forearm. Not to touch his shoulder to make a point. She couldn't take her eyes off him, even in their picturesque surroundings.

Her memories may never return. It had been nearly four weeks since the accident. Over three since she'd regained consciousness. She knew that the more days that passed, the less likely it was her memories would return. She had to get on with this new life.

So instead of trying to remember what their relationship had been like, she had to forge a new one. She wasn't sure exactly what that relationship looked like, but she was hoping it involved them being more than just friends.

Nico looked around the village of Tregua, hoping to see something familiar. But it was all different. Some things were bigger, some smaller. And the most important things were not there at all.

It shouldn't have surprised him; it had been over twenty years since he was last here and even though so much about this place had not changed in millennia, everything felt different. Only one thing was the same. The smell. Every place in the world had its unique scent, and Tregua was no different.

Lemon. Dust. Salty air. Frying fish.

The house Anna still lived in was a short walk away. Or so he thought. The village was set around a small circular harbour. The fishing boats were tied up as they always were in the late morning, back from the dawn trip. The ancient houses were painted white so the whole place sparkled in the sun. The part of the town where they had lived was close to the water and the fishing docks.

'Oh, Nico, it's gorgeous.'

You're gorgeous, he wanted to say, but instead went with the far more sensible 'Anna's house is a street back from the sea.'

'Yes, just round the corner from the main square with the church,' she said and they both stopped walking.

She was right.

'How did you know that?'

'I don't know. Didn't you say?'

He had indeed told her; he had described the village to her several times when they were planning the book and the trip. But that had all been before the accident.

'We talked about it, but that was a while ago.'

Even he was struggling to reconcile his childhood memories with this place, she remembered.

Her face became brighter than he'd seen it in weeks. Her beautiful eyes were wide and excited. Pink colour bloomed high on her cheeks. His heart rate hitched.

'Do you remember anything else?'

She looked around frantically, as though searching for a lost item so she could leave the house. Kids ran around with a shiny brown labrador, and several elderly men sat on wooden chairs in the shade. Her face closed over and she shook her head.

'Sometimes I don't know what is real and what isn't,' she said and he understood so completely he couldn't help but pick up her hand.

It was what he'd wanted to do, what he'd longed to do for years: walk through this village holding her hand, knowing she was with him and that the past didn't matter.

For a brief moment he gave in to the longing and let himself believe that dream was still possible. Hand in hand with Freya, back here, and everyone was alright. His father, his mother. And Freya. He indulged that fantasy for few minutes only, then pulled his thoughts back to reality.

'Forget me and my faulty memory for a moment. You spent the first ten years of your life here. What do *you* remember?'

'Feelings, mostly. Smells. Tastes.'

That was why the cookbook was so important. It would be a way of bringing back his parents in some little way. A tribute to them. And it was also why it had taken him so long to come back here and do this. It was only with Freya's gentle encouragement that he'd felt brave enough.

And now? Even though she was here, holding his hand, it was far from what he'd imagined.

'I remember certain things, but I don't know how they fit together. A kitchen. A bedroom. A garden. But I don't know if they belonged to the same house.'

She grinned. 'I sometimes feel like that too. I recall disjointed images, but I don't know if they go together or the order they came in. Or even if they're real.'

'Exactly.' He couldn't have put it better himself. He squeezed her hand.

When they reached the point where the entire bay came into view, he stopped.

'This is it,' he whispered.

The bay glistened blue and turquoise, belying the tragedy that had happened here.

'It's beautiful,' she said.

'This is the bay where my father died,' he said before he could stop himself.

'Oh, Nico. Here? I'm so sorry.'

It had been a bright day, just like now. Clear and calm. It had been a freak accident.

'I should have been able to do something.'

'Nico, what? No! You were five. It can't have been your fault.'

He shook his head. 'I could've done more.'

'I'm sure no one could have prevented it. There would've been other people around. Adults. Everyone would have done everything they could.'

She could try to comfort him as much as she wanted, but he knew. He'd been there. He'd seen it.

He turned from the water, still holding her hand, like the life raft that should have come for his father.

Tourism had become one of the biggest industries in Puglia in recent years, but it was barely encroaching on Tregua, which remained primarily a fishing village.

He glanced around, from the street that led to the square, down to the docks.

'The restaurant is down that way.' He pointed down to the boat sheds. The restaurant, which had been in a converted shed, was directly on the water. 'The only place you can get fresher seafood is on the boat itself.'

Freya tugged on his hand. 'Your father used to say that.'

Nico stopped and closed his eyes as a rush of emotion surged through him. Even though it was a statement, not a question, he still said, 'Yes.'

He'd told her that many times. In fact, he recalled his father's words anytime he was lucky enough to eat seafood by the water.

'Did I remember that as well?'

He nodded.

It turned out today was a big one for both their memories.

'Our house was just this way.' He turned down a lane.

'Is it still there?' she asked.

'I honestly don't know. But most of these buildings are at least a hundred years old so we'll see.'

'Are you okay to go to your house?' she asked.

'Yes, it's why I came, after all.'

'But it's still hard.' She squeezed his hand and he longed to twirl her entire body to his.

They walked slowly down the laneway, taking in everything. The kids running past them, the occasional Vespa speeding by. People going about their days.

And there it was.

He stopped and she did too, studying it as he did. A single-storey cottage, so much smaller than in his memories. A blue door, a single window at the front and whitewashed like most of the other cottages.

'Do you want to knock?' she asked. 'Say hello? Tell them who you are?'

What would be the point? It would be different and muddle his memories. Or it would be the same and that would somehow be even worse.

'Not just yet.' He'd wait until the lump in his chest was not as large, not as unpredictable. 'It's still standing' he said, stating the obvious.

'Is that good or bad?'

'Good, I think. I'd have been devastated to find

my childhood home knocked down. But it's still strange.'

This village might have been his home. If his parents had lived, he had little doubt he would have followed them into the business, stayed in this village his entire life.

And you'd have never met Freya.

But he also wouldn't have nearly killed her.

CHAPTER SIX

WHAT A DAY they were having and it wasn't even lunchtime.

Nico was overwhelmed with childhood memories and emotions and she was ill equipped to help him, with her own memories fighting their way to the surface in odd and unexpected ways.

They must have spoken so much about this place; why else would she have remembered something as random as the directions to Nico's childhood home? Just her luck to remember Nico's past when she couldn't even remember what she'd been doing two months ago.

No. It was more than that. She was remembering things that Nico had told her. She was remembering a story she had been told. A story that was close to her heart. It was important.

Tregua was Nico's hometown and it had somehow formed part of her memories, yet she'd never been here. How was that possible?

They went to find Anna's house next.

'You've kept in touch with her?'

He pulled a face. 'I tried to. We wrote occasionally but I was a pretty typical teenage boy and not a great pen pal. And it was hard, being in London. Each time I'd try to write I'd have to think about this place and…it wasn't always easy. But she still lives in the same house she always did.'

'And even though you kept up your spoken Italian you lost the confidence to write.'

They both stopped walking and her throat felt as though it was closing over. She shouldn't know that. She looked to Nico for confirmation.

He squeezed her hand. 'Yes, exactly.'

She was suddenly conscious that his hand was still wrapped around hers. Warm, reassuring. The really strange thing was that it didn't feel unusual. Did they usually hold hands? She understood they were close friends, but what sort of friendship involved walking around holding hands and nothing more? Not a purely platonic one.

They walked past a small market in the square, a fraction of the size of the one they had visited in Bari, with one butcher, two fishmongers and three vegetable stalls.

'The church looks different because it was built by the Byzantines,' he said.

'Yes, but the rest was built by the Venetians. The whole region is very rich in history. The Greeks, Romans, even the Normans. So many civilisations have stamped their mark on this place.' She stopped, heart in her throat. She'd done it again. California Freya couldn't have pointed to Puglia on a map, but London Freya knew its history.

More information had popped into her head from nowhere.

No, it came from somewhere. It came from you. You knew all of this stuff.

Nico no longer seemed to notice; his eyes were drawn to one of the small streets leading away from the square.

Anna was sitting outside waiting for them. The woman squinted when she saw Nico, needing to reconcile the ten-year-old she'd known with the gorgeous grown man walking towards her, but Nico knew immediately.

'Anna!'

They hugged and she held his cheeks to examine him, then hugged him again.

Freya stood back and watched but was soon drawn into an embrace as well.

'*Bella* Freya! Welcome!'

They were ushered into the house, through to the kitchen. Delicious smells emanated from a steaming pot on the stove.

Colourful cast iron pots—a food stylist's dream—hung from the walls. It was a casual, relaxed kitchen that looked lived-in and loved. For generations.

Freya didn't know much Italian but could pick up a few words. Nico translated now and then, but she didn't need to know every word to understand what the conversation was about. They talked about his life in London, his restaurants. Once they'd finished eating and were mopping their bowls with the fresh bread, the conversation changed to his parents. Nico brushed away some tears but Anna let hers flow freely.

'She's telling me how much she loved them both, how she still misses them. What a tragedy it was.'

Freya didn't need a translation; everything was clear from Anna's tears.

Anna then picked up some framed photographs and showed them both. Nico explained that they were of her children and grandchildren.

After a while the topic of conversation changed again, but this time Nico made no effort to translate and he looked uneasy.

Freya could tell by the way Anna kept looking from her to Nico and back again that they were talking about her. Nico said something and Anna let out a sharp laugh and shook her head vigorously.

'What's going on?' Freya muttered to Nico.

'It doesn't matter.' He shook his head and Anna laughed again.

It clearly did matter. Nico's face was burning.

Anna grabbed Freya's hand and said, '*Bella, Bella.*' Followed by some more Italian that was far beyond Freya's progress on her language app.

She's asked him about our relationship.

With much of her memory missing, Freya was getting very proficient at piecing things together with context clues alone. By the way Nico's face was now the colour of one of the jars of home-made tomato sauce on Anna's shelf, Freya knew Anna had asked something personal.

She's asking about our relationship and he's blushing.

But what did it mean? She wanted to yell. What was he saying and what was the truth?

What are we to one another?

Freya had chosen a beautiful hotel for them in Monopoli. It was perched on one of the limestone cliffs and their adjoining rooms overlooked the turquoise waters. She knocked on the door between their rooms and opened it slowly.

'Have you seen this view?' She opened her arms. 'We can actually smell the ocean.'

He could feel her excitement in his chest. 'You chose this place.'

'I have good taste.' She grinned.

'You do,' he said but with a serious tone. It was wonderful to see her confidence returning. She might be remembering the past in strange and random glimpses, but the main thing that had changed about her since arriving in Italy was that she was less timid, less hesitant.

Less worried. Much of her anxiety and fear

seemed to have been left behind in London. Her true personality was beginning to shine and that was better than any memories returning.

'Anyway,' she said, ignoring his compliment. 'Do I have time for a swim before dinner? The hotel has a pool.'

'Sure, this is Italy, remember—everyone eats late.'

Freya shot him a wide smile and disappeared back into her room, closing the door behind her.

He wasn't just warm. He was hot. And felt itchy under his skin. A swim seemed like the best idea he'd heard all day.

Except when he arrived at the pool deck fifteen minutes later it was to find Freya lifting a loose dress over her head to reveal a red bikini. The fabric stretched over her body like it had been woven around her curves. The swimsuit wasn't immodest, but certainly not substantial enough to be providing much support. Not that she needed that. Freya's body was perfectly stunning. In or out of clothes.

Or red string bikinis.

As soon as her face appeared out of the dress, she caught him looking at her.

Like a thief.

'Hey,' he said quickly. 'A swim sounded like a good idea. I hope you don't mind me joining you?'

'I, um, no. Of course not.'

He dropped his towel on the lounger next to

hers and took his T-shirt off as fast as he could. Then as quickly as he decently could he jumped into the pool before she could see exactly how much he liked the red bikini. The water was refreshing after the long day and the drive, but was not quite cold enough to dull the throbbing in his veins he had each time he looked at Freya.

An ice bath wouldn't have been enough.

She swam some lazy laps, not making eye contact with him, and left the water first. The water dripping from her bikini-clad body reminded him of the morning after *that* night. He had to remain in the pool a while longer, thinking about the least sexy things he could imagine before he could safely climb out. He was conscious his wet shorts would cling to his body and hide very little.

He dipped his head below the surface, and when he emerged, he faced away from her. He gave her a few minutes to dry off and when he looked in her direction again, she was wearing the white cotton dress and was stretched out on the lounger.

He sighed with relief and pulled himself out of the pool, not exactly cooled off but certainly cooler than he'd been thirty minutes ago.

You've had an emotional day, that's all.

He'd visited Tregua and Anna and talked about his parents with someone who had known and loved them both. No wonder he wasn't able to control himself; he'd had a very stressful day.

He wrapped a towel around his waist and perched on the lounger next to Freya's.

'What were you and Anna talking about?' she asked.

'I'm sorry I couldn't translate everything.'

'There's no need to apologise—it was *your* visit. I'm honoured you took me with you.'

She sounded so honest and earnest and of course he'd taken her with him. There was no one else in the world he'd wanted to take with him on this trip, and particularly on that visit.

He was so churned up inside. So many memories were rising back into his conscious thoughts. Some things he'd purposely tried to forget because it was so much easier to look forward and not back. Many other memories had been unintended casualties of suppressing the bad memories. And so many things he'd simply forgotten. Today they'd all come up to hit him in the face.

'We talked about her family. She has four kids, and they have kids of their own. Most still live in Tregua or here in Monopoli.'

'Wonderful.'

It was. It made him wonder, not for the first time that day, what his life would have been like if his father hadn't died, if the three of them had stayed in Puglia. What would he have become? Would he have joined his father on the fishing boats or his mother in the kitchen? Or done something else entirely?

One thing was certain: he never would have met Freya. Either way, a whole lot of hurt would have been avoided if he'd been able to act faster on the day his father died.

Everyone's lives would've been different.

'She suggested I go down to see the restaurant.'

'Will you?'

'I know I should but…'

'It would be hard.'

For an instant he saw her again, the woman who understood him without him having to explain himself. His Freya.

She's not yours.

He had to keep reminding himself. They were not together and never could be. Even if he could see the outline of the red bikini through the white dress, now transparent from the water. Even then.

Freya looked at him with a wry smile. 'She asked you if we are together, didn't she?'

Caught again.

'Not exactly.'

'Then what exactly?'

'She asked us *why* we're not together. Totally different thing.'

Freya raised a single, perfect eyebrow.

'Why *did* we never get together?'

His rib cage tightened around his heart and lungs. Sitting next to her now, with her outrageously sexy bikini clearly visible through her wet white dress, he honestly had no idea.

They should be up in his room, lying together on his bed, with him peeling her bikini off with his teeth, her long fingers edging down his shorts…

Because you messed it all up. That's why you're not together and never will be.

'We're friends, colleagues.'

She nodded as if she also knew that was the official reason.

But not the real reason.

'Are you in love with someone else?' she asked.

Her question nearly made his heart stop beating.

'Someone else?' he choked.

She crinkled up her face. 'Yes.'

Was he in love with someone else?

How could he have been when for as long as he could remember it had only been her? Stolen glances, guilty longings. Repressed desires. He knew they could never be together. There was too much between them and too much at stake, but that didn't mean that he didn't wonder.

'No. Freya, it's like I said. We're good friends and colleagues. We had—have—something really good. We never wanted to mess up the good thing we had going, I guess.'

She nodded again, but it wasn't the nod of someone who agreed but of someone who knew they weren't being told everything.

'I'd better get ready for dinner,' he said and stood. 'See you around seven?'

'Yes.' She smiled up at him and his stupid heart broke all over again.

He walked away but as he got to the corner he glanced back. She was still sitting on the lounger, her knees tucked up and her arms hugging her legs. Her face was resting on her knees.

He couldn't tell her what had happened, but he couldn't keep not telling her.

We never wanted to mess up the good thing we had going.

Until the night before the accident, when they had.

The night before her thirtieth birthday. It was only a few weeks ago but he'd lived a lifetime since then.

Nico had planned a surprise party for Freya at the restaurant for the following night, the night of her birthday. They were closing the place for the evening. He and the rest of the team wanted to show her how much she meant to them. Lately she'd seemed restless and he'd wanted to lift her spirits. He was excited, but anxious that she'd find out about the party and it wouldn't be a surprise. He'd been excited about Italy, about the coming weeks and months, but also sensed somehow that Freya was worried about something. He couldn't put his finger on why she was unsettled and she wouldn't say. He put it down to the fact that significant birthdays often stir up thoughts of change within people.

That night he'd arrived home around nine, after he'd assured himself the dinner service was going smoothly. Freya was home before him and waiting for him in the living room. She was wearing her favourite boots, but with a gorgeous pink silky dress he hadn't seen before. The neckline dipped lower than she usually wore it, and he averted his eyes to the spread on the coffee table next to the sofa. There were wineglasses and a plate of cheeses and crackers, though he didn't want to eat anything after she told him her news.

She was leaving.

'Back to California?'

'I just need a change.'

'From what?

She told him she'd been thinking about her future as a major birthday approached, just as he'd thought.

'I want more.'

'What could be more than this? The life we have here, the business we've been building?'

'I love my job. I love my life here, but I need more.'

More. That word again.

'A pay rise? Name your price.'

She smiled and shook her head. 'It's not about that.'

She clenched and unclenched her hands and

then said softly, 'I need to know what I will mean to you in the future.'

It felt as though something had reached up from inside him and squeezed his gut. Nervous, sickening.

The question he had always been most afraid she'd ask.

She wasn't talking about another trip or writing another book. She wasn't even talking about opening another restaurant.

She was talking about something far, far bigger. It was a conversation he'd occasionally think about, and then shut down that thought. Because the idea of what she was talking about was scary enough but the reality? He'd be risking everything.

'I'm about to be thirty, and one day—I'm not saying it has to be tomorrow—but one day I'd like to get married and have a family.'

He adored Freya. She was the most fun, happiest, most integral part of his life. And if things had been different, if *he* had been different, then he may have already told her all this and they would already be embarking on the journey she was talking about: love, romance, a family.

Some days it took every ounce of his self-control not to reach out to her.

Not to tell her how much he wanted her.

He'd made it through the past few years with

much selective blindness...and many, many cold showers and long runs.

He loved Freya, but it was precisely because he thought so much of her that they couldn't be together. Not romantically. She was his best friend.

'Do you ever think about us?' she whispered.

Constantly, consistently and mostly chastely. Because when I think of more it all becomes too confusing.

'Of course I do.'

Her eyes opened wide. 'And?'

'And we work together. And live together. And you're my best friend.'

'I know, and it's wonderful and I'm probably crazy to put it all on the line, but I want more, Nico. With you. And I want to know if you think there's even a chance that you might too.'

'Of course I do.' Despite trying otherwise, his words were full of pain. He wanted her, but he couldn't have her. What if he lost her? What if something happened to her? What if he hurt her too?

'You do?' Her beautiful forehead creased. 'You don't sound particularly happy about it.'

'Freya, you're my person. I adore you. Of course I think about you. About us.'

'But?'

'I'm your boss.' That was the truth, but just the start of what lay between them.

'I'll quit.'

He laughed. 'Freya, I'm not going to let you give up your career for me.'

Even if she didn't work for him, there were still so many reasons why changing the nature of their relationship was a bad idea.

He drew a deep breath and turned to face her properly and explain that a romantic relationship would only lead to heartache. Or worse.

But somehow when he turned, the cushion next to him sunk and his hand brushed against hers in the dip between them. They'd touched before. They'd hugged many times. And each time he'd been prepared. Or they hadn't been in the middle of a conversation like this and he'd been able to quell the sparks and bury the desire back away where it belonged.

But this time he simply hadn't been able to.

He dragged his fingertips across her knuckles. The most sensitive part of his hand brushed against the least sensitive of hers. A wave of heat whispered through him, but her eyes widened, irises open. Alert.

Seeing her reaction, his eyes widened as well. Thoughts opened, clicked into place, like a row of doors all unlocking at once.

He couldn't lose her! He couldn't let her go. He couldn't live without her. And not because she was his friend, not because she was his most trusted colleague, but because he didn't want to go a day without seeing her first thing in the morning.

And his entire body began to shake at the thought of going to bed each night for the rest of his life without the comfort of knowing she was asleep under the same roof as him.

He closed his eyes and leaned towards her. Their noses brushed, their breath mingled but still he held back from the line he was moving towards. The line he knew he shouldn't cross.

Freya's breathing quickened and his heart beat in his throat. He didn't want her to go but couldn't give her what she was asking.

Yet how could he pull himself away?

He rested his unopened mouth against hers, breathed in the same air, pausing on the edge. Even when he ran a hand up her smooth arm, he didn't open his mouth and neither did she.

He felt her sigh, heard her whimper. Only then did he finally open his mouth, causing her to open hers, sliding into one another, coming together.

And then she kissed him and he was lost.

And then everything went wrong.

Their evening in Monopoli followed the same pattern as the night before: drinks and nibbles at a bar, followed by dinner at a nearby restaurant where Nico ordered a variety of dishes and they both tried all of them. It was decadent and delicious and once again she was jealous of herself and the life she'd been living for the past few years. It seemed so wonderful that sometimes she almost wanted to laugh out loud.

But it wasn't all perfect. Right now, they were in a picture-perfect restaurant, enjoying a spread of mouth-watering food, attention from the staff. They could talk about the food and the view but not about what was really worrying her.

Nico could give her all the excuses he wanted to—*We're good friends, We don't want to ruin a good thing*—but she'd seen the way he looked at her. She'd seen his reaction to her bikini earlier, she'd noticed the look on his face when he thought she wasn't looking and she knew there was something he wasn't telling her.

She wanted to scream at him to tell her, but then she remembered the promise she'd asked him and her mother to make: don't tell me about past lovers, I don't want to know.

But she hadn't meant *him*.

Or had she?

What if he did tell her yes, they'd been lovers? Yes, they had slept together. How would she process that? Particularly when every time she saw him, she wanted to touch him, reach for him, taste him.

This afternoon, by the pool, she'd almost had to look away as he climbed out of the pool. His chest was broad, flat and bronzed. Slick with the water from the pool, glistening in the setting sun.

As chiselled as his jaw, as well defined as his cheekbones. The man was all smooth surfaces, sharp lines and soft shadows. She salivated, and not because of the magnificent desserts laid out on the table before them, but because of the man across from her, licking his lips and half closing his eyes as he tasted them.

Besides, did it matter if they had been lovers if she couldn't remember? Wouldn't it be better to create some new memories, ones that were not lost?

Freya decided to try a little experiment with the *limoncello* semifreddo. She heaped her fork inelegantly with a too-big serving and made sure it missed her mouth. She licked most of it away but was confident she'd left a smudge just next to her lips.

She continued the conversation without missing a beat, but Nico's attention began to drift and he was staring at the food she'd left on her face.

'You, um, you've got some cream on your face.'

'Oh, embarrassing,' she said and used her napkin to wipe the right side of her lips. 'Better?'

'No, it's on the left.'

She wiped the left-hand side of her face but deliberately missed the food.

'Now?' she asked, feigning confusion.

'No, it's…' He waved to her face and again she attempted to wipe it away, deliberately missing again.

Nico leaned forward. She closed her eyes and moved in. She inhaled as deeply as she could and as she felt his thumb brush against the delicate skin next to her lips she opened her eyes, meeting his gaze in a flash. His pupils widened and he inhaled sharply. His brown versus her blue, locked for a moment in a deep, entangled gaze. With a quick movement he wiped her mouth clean and sat back, as though he'd been scalded.

'Thanks,' he murmured.

Her heart was racing.

He looked at his plate and pushed his food around for a few minutes.

What was wrong with this man?

This wasn't how platonic friends behaved, was it? Accelerating heart rates, shortness of breath, dilating pupils?

No. It wasn't.

Their friendship might be platonic on his side, but it wasn't on hers. If there were reasons they weren't together, she didn't remember them. And what if her memory never came back? She couldn't wait around to find out. So what if London Freya was too scared to take their relationship to the next level? This Freya, Italy Freya, had only just survived a life-threatening accident.

Italy Freya knew how precious life was, how precious memories were. Italy Freya wasn't worried about preserving a friendship she couldn't remember, or a job she didn't even know how to do. Italy Freya only knew one thing for sure: that when she looked into the chocolate brown eyes of the beautiful man across the table from her, her insides turned molten, just like her heart.

Their hotel was a short walk along the wall of the old fort, by the sea. On their walk back, she stopped and pointed across the bay to the twinkling lights beyond.

'It's gorgeous. Thank you for letting me come here with you.'

Nico stopped walking too. Freya took a deep breath, turned and stepped up to him, holding his gaze in hers. He looked down at her, eyes full of confusion, but the unmistakable heaviness of longing.

'What? What is it?' he asked.

At this moment, overlooking the Adriatic, there was only him. There was no friendship that she remembered, no career she felt she needed to protect. Only Nico. The only memory that mattered was of him sitting by the pool, his bare chest glistening with drops of water in the sunlight. Of him looking at her longingly when he thought she wasn't noticing. Of him brushing her lips when she had cream on them.

She took his hand in hers. He looked down but didn't snatch his away. That was a good sign. She squeezed. He squeezed back and an ache of longing spread through her body.

She mustered every seduction tool she had and

stepped closer. Only a breath separated their bodies, so close she could feel the heat emanating from him. Freya slipped her tongue oh so briefly over her bottom lip and was rewarded by his pupils expanding to the edges of his irises.

Why was he fighting this? It was clear to everyone in a ten-mile radius that they were attracted to one another. The magnetism was probably throwing out all the nearby compasses.

Usually by this point the guy had taken all the hints she'd laid down, but Nico was unbreakable. Stoic even. The muscles in his jaw tightened and he pursed his lips together.

'Look, we're friends, right?' she said.

'The best.'

'Then please tell me something honestly.'

He nodded slightly, as though in agreement, though hardly happy at the prospect.

'Are you attracted to me?'

He coughed. 'What kind of question is that?'

'A real one. An honest one. Because I'm attracted to you. I have been since the first time I laid eyes on you and I just don't understand.'

He cleared his throat again. 'What don't you understand?'

'I don't understand how I did this for five years! How we were next to one another every day and we never kissed.' *Because kissing you is all I can think about.*

Nico closed his eyes tight, as though blocking something out. As though he was in pain.

'We never came close? Never touched one another?'

'Freya, please.'

She felt his frustration in her gut but it only propelled her forward. She slid her palm up his forearm, pushing the hair against its natural direction. She cupped his elbow in her hand.

'We never did this?'

He winced but she was no longer expecting an answer. At least not a truthful one.

'What about this?'

Her hand continued its journey up his hard, muscular arm and her fingers slipped under the hem of his shirt sleeve, to the soft skin beneath it. It was like the finest velvet beneath her fingertips and she stroked her fingertips in small circles, loving the sensation on her skin, as well as the clear frustration creasing his brow.

'Because it seems like such a shame. Such a waste,' she whispered.

He tensed further beneath her touch, but didn't step back or even pull away. His breathing was as ragged as hers.

Freya slid her hand across his arm and to his chest, where it came to rest at the neckline of his shirt. Her fingers were safely resting on the linen fabric, but her thumb brushed ever so lightly against the sensitive skin just below his throat.

Nico let out one last grunt of frustration and the next thing she knew he'd pressed his lips to hers. No ceremony, no hesitation—his mouth was open and his tongue was seeking out hers. She opened her mouth and her arms and met him with the same fervour. Rushed, hot, insatiable. Desperate. Like he needed her to breathe.

He held her in his arms, pulled her to him, slid one hand expertly up her neck, into her hair and tilted her head just perfectly so as to give his lips maximum coverage of hers.

Everything started to fall around her—her knees, her inhibitions, the world—but he held her close and tight, even as she felt his body shake against hers.

His kisses became shorter, his breath rough.

She pulled back, panting, head spinning. 'I guess that's my answer.'

Nico stepped back, the realisation of what he'd just done hitting him again and again. She could see from the look on his face he'd done the very thing he'd been fighting against. The very thing he'd clearly vowed not to do.

'I'm sorry.'

She held up her hand. 'Uh, you have nothing to be sorry about. I'm the one who unleashed that.'

That.

Uncontrolled, runaway passion.

It was no wonder he'd tried to keep that in its box. Desire like that had a power all its own.

And then she knew.

She may not have remembered, but she *knew.*

He had kissed her before.

Those were not the actions of a couple doing it for the first time. They were the movements of a couple who had been trying not to do that for an even longer time. He was not kissing like a man who had never once thought about kissing her.

She took his hand and silently started to walk the short distance to the hotel, body still vibrating, blood thumping, thoughts swimming in one, single direction. Directly towards Nico's bed.

His hand was loose in hers; she was conscious she was practically dragging him along with her. But she didn't care. There was a doorway up ahead and she was going to pull them through it before it closed.

The street outside the hotel was deserted. She paused at the entrance.

'Come to my room.'

'Freya, I can't.'

'Why not?'

'Because it's too complicated.' He screwed up his eyes, closing them to her and all the possibilities that were so clear to her.

'Maybe it was once, but I'm not that Freya anymore. I know that life can change in an instant. I know how precious it is and how you have to live every moment.'

'And that's exactly why. Because life is precious and I don't want to ruin it.'

'I'm not scared of ruining a friendship I can't remember.'

He groaned. 'It's more than that.'

'Why? What is it? I know there's something you're not telling me.'

He took both her hands in his and drew a deep breath. Her heart swelled at his earnestness, at the way his eyes softened at the edges. 'I don't want to hurt you,' he said.

That was not what she was expecting him to say. 'I don't want to hurt you either. But I don't see how sleeping with me will hurt either of us.'

'Because it *will.*'

Not the way I do it, she almost said, but didn't think this brand of humour would be welcome when Nico was clearly struggling with something.

'But why?'

'Because it already has. I can't do relationships.'

She wanted to laugh, but the look in his eyes stopped her. He didn't 'do' relationships? What did that mean? What kind of clichéd line was that from a man who was anything but? His glare warned her otherwise. Whatever his reasons were, London Freya, as his best friend, clearly understood them. This Freya was suddenly on uncertain, even dangerous ground.

If he didn't do relationships, then why had he

kissed her before? Not just now, but the other time, that time her body remembered but her brain steadfastly refused to acknowledge.

She opened her mouth to confront him with her suspicions but stopped mid-breath. She had asked him not to tell her about past boyfriends. They'd sat with her mother at their kitchen table and she had made him promise not to tell her about her past lovers.

I need to remember that sort of thing myself.

Besides, they were not a couple. Everyone had been clear on that topic and she didn't get the feeling that Nico would lie about something like that. Or that everyone else would too.

If they had kissed before, if they had slept together, then they had also broken up.

And she wasn't sure she wanted to hear about *that.* It was enough to still be getting her head around Jane and Lachlan; she didn't want to know that Nico had also dumped her. She wanted to take him to her room and forget that London Freya had ever existed. Now it was just them. The two of them, this night.

But she didn't make a move.

She could barely make sense of her thoughts when Nico said, 'Good night.'

'Yes, good night.'

He stepped towards the doors. When she didn't follow, he turned.

'You go ahead. I just need a moment.'

He looked up and down the street, as if assessing whether it was wise.

'I'll be fine. Go!'

He lingered for a moment, clearly unhappy about it, but the street was quiet, the town more so. She needed air. The thought of going up to her room, with Nico's room right next door, was a little too stifling.

Freya walked down to the corner and the wall overlooking the water. She breathed in the smell of the sea, the salt and the night air.

There was something familiar about the smell that she couldn't quite place. Smell and taste were often so evocative. Jane's perfume, her mother's fabric conditioner, her grandmother's house. All familiar smells guaranteed to bring memories to the surface.

And this smell.

She sniffed her jacket.

No. Not the sea, but Nico. The smell was Nico on her. His lips, his skin, just the merest of scents left behind on her.

She breathed in it again, hoping for all the answers to come, but they didn't.

Stupid, stupid brain. Stupid accident.

What on earth did 'I can't do relationships' mean?

Because it already has.

Something hit her—not a memory, but a realisation.

Because it already has.

He'd been talking about them. He meant that he'd hurt her in the past and he didn't want to do so again. He had broken up with her. No wonder he didn't want to tell her everything. Suddenly everything was so much more complicated than it had been ten minutes ago.

Hours later, asleep in bed, a sound woke Freya. Deep, pained, primal.

Was it inside? Outside? An animal. What animals were there in Puglia that made such a sound?

Freya sat up and looked around the room, her eyes adjusting to the light. She heard it again. A low moan. Someone in pain. And it wasn't coming from outside, but from next door. Nico's room. She swung her legs off the side of the bed and stepped onto the cool marble floor. Could she just barge in?

She turned on her bedside light and waited. Then she heard it again.

'Mama. Mama.'

Deciding there was something very wrong, she pushed open the door to his adjoining room, grateful he hadn't been so angry with her about the kiss as to lock it.

'Nico, Nico. Are you okay?'

Just enough light was creeping into his room from hers to allow her to make out him in his bed, tossing from one side to the other.

'Mama?' This time it was a question and it broke her heart into pieces.

'Nico, sweetheart, you need to wake up.' She had no idea where the 'sweetheart' part had come from but it seemed to do the trick. He woke with a gasp and a grunt.

'Nico, it's just me. Freya. Are you okay?'

He sat up abruptly, grabbed at his bed for something that wasn't there, then finally focused on her.

'I'm sorry, I didn't mean to wake you. Except yes, I guess I did. You sounded so distressed,' she said.

Recognition, realisation crept over his face and he fell back onto his pillows and groaned again. This was a different groan, though, laced with embarrassment and frustration.

Freya looked around the room, picked up an empty water glass and filled it in the bathroom sink. She handed it to Nico, who eyed her and the glass sceptically before sitting up again and accepting it.

He was shirtless and wearing goodness knows what under the sheet. She was suddenly conscious of the thin, strappy singlet and shorts she had on.

'I'm sorry I woke you,' he said.

'I'm sorry about whatever was happening to you in that dream.'

'No, I'm sorry.'

'Don't be silly. I was looking for an excuse to

get into your room. You know that.' She smiled, hoping he appreciated the joke.

He smiled and she relaxed a little. They would be okay.

'The joke's on me, I guess.'

He patted the edge of his bed and she sat at the foot. She resisted the desire to sit at waist level and slide her arms around him. Climb on top of him.

'What was your dream about?'

'The same as usual.'

'Which is?'

'My mother…my father.'

'Oh.'

'It's strange being here in ways I hadn't anticipated. I've dreamed about them every night. Sometimes they're happy dreams—we're sitting at our kitchen table or playing with our dog or at the beach.'

'I'm guessing this one wasn't one of those.'

'No. It was my mother. It was the day she died.'

'Oh, Nico.' Freya wanted to hug him but settled for reaching out to the closest body part, his lower leg, and rested her hand on it.

'I don't know what's wrong with me.'

'Nothing's wrong with you! It's completely normal to be feeling like this being back here. I've been doing lots of reading about memory, funnily enough. Everything I've read suggests going back to places that were meaningful is likely to bring things to the surface. Places, smells, people all act as triggers. Coming here may not have been doing much for my memory loss, but it's stirring up all sorts of things in you. It's understandable.'

He shook his head. 'I knew bringing you here was a bad idea.'

'Nonsense. I *have* been remembering things, here and there. You know that.'

And everything I've remembered relates to you.

'My memory will come in time.' And because it was dark and because he'd already shared things with her she said, 'To be honest, I'm starting wonder if I want my memories back.'

'Why?' Nico sat straighter, pulled his legs and the sheets around him, but at the same time leaned forward.

I'm scared to know what happened between us.

'I'm scared about what I've forgotten. I'm worried that I must have blocked them for some reason.' *I'm worried you broke my heart and that's the thing my brain doesn't want to remember.*

He dropped his head. 'No, I've told you. You were happy. You were well. You were not distressed.'

And yet he'd hurt her. And something *had* happened between them. Her brain might not have remembered but her body did.

'You said I was thinking of my next steps on my birthday. What did you mean?'

'Ah. You weren't unhappy. I promise. You were thinking about moving back to California.'

'I was?'

'I didn't want you to. I *don't* want you to.'

And yet?

'You said it was because you were turning thirty. Thinking about your next steps, whether they would be in London. Or the States. Or somewhere else.'

'Did I have something lined up?'

'I don't think so, no, but Freya, you were never short of offers. You'd get one or two a week from people trying to poach you.'

'I did?'

He laughed. 'You did. More than anything, I truly hope you remember how great you are at your job.'

Nico leaned forward further and Freya realised she had as well. His knees and a white sheet were all that separated them. His gaze dropped and she saw it land on her pyjama singlet, which left very little to the imagination. She held her breath.

A second later, Nico realised where he was and what he was looking at and shuffled back on the bed. 'I'm sorry again for waking you.'

She shook her head. 'Don't mention it. Are you alright now?'

'I'm fine,' he said, though she wasn't sure she believed him.

CHAPTER SEVEN

NICO STRUGGLED TO get back to sleep after his midnight talk with Freya.

He lay awake, staring at the ceiling. The slowly turning fan was not enough to hypnotise him back to sleep. When the sunlight began to creep in around the shutters he gave up, got up and showered. His mind was a tangle of the dream that had woken him and Freya, barely clothed, sitting at the end of his bed, resting her hand gently on his leg but sending sparks all through his body.

And of course, the kiss. The kiss he'd been helpless to avoid and unable to stop. The kiss that had excited him and terrified him in equal measure.

She would remember eventually. Snippets of her memories had been returning to her all day. About Tregua. About his home.

Most worrying of all, even if she'd forgotten the details of their relationship, she hadn't forgotten the one thing he really needed her to: her attraction to him.

He had to tell her.

Tell her what? You made love and then you crashed the car?

The voice in his head scolding him he should have told her already was getting louder and louder. It was only just overruled by the fact she had told him she didn't want to hear about her ex-lovers, that she needed to remember things like that on her own.

But when did protecting her become lying?

Freya's room was still quiet by the time he'd dressed. The only firm plans for the day were for later in the morning. He slipped a note under her door and then set off alone.

The early-morning streets were already bustling with locals going about their day and the market was already in full swing, but he set off in the other direction, away from the sea, away from the centre of the old town. Searching for something though he wasn't sure what.

Freya was exactly right about his dream. It was understandable he'd been flooded with memories of his parents since he'd arrived back in Puglia. It had literally been one of the aims of the trip: to remember the food from his childhood. He'd anticipated the seafood, the orecchiette and the *panzerotto*, but he hadn't anticipated dreaming about being in his mother's hospital room as she passed away. Or what returning to the place where he'd watched his father drown would do to his already shaky equilibrium.

This was the reason he'd avoided returning here for so long. While he'd been to other parts of Italy, he seemed to know on some level that coming back to Puglia, and Tregua in particular, would be difficult.

It was Freya who had gently encouraged the trip, suggesting every now and then that it would be good for him. He'd thought she meant that it would be a good business opportunity, a good series and book to write, but he now wondered if she'd had something deeper in mind.

It was only with her support and the knowledge that she'd be with him every step of the way that he'd agreed to the trip. But, of course, since then everything had changed. He was now looking after Freya and dealing with the guilt of that accident.

No wonder he was also being tortured with nightmares from his past. Being in his mother's hospital room as she struggled for breath, standing alone by the harbour, frozen to the spot as the boat sunk. Unable to yell.

He shook himself back to the present. He had to focus on why he was here in the first place. It wasn't to worry incessantly about Freya, and it certainly wasn't to kiss her. It also wasn't to be sad about his parents; he had come here to *work*. To research his next book. His next series. To decide what he was going to write about and what recipes of Puglia he would showcase.

At the thought of food, even despite the churning in his gut, his stomach predictably rumbled. Freya had researched a range of places she wanted them to try, but he wasn't with Freya. He was alone.

Nico looked through the window of a nearby cafe. It looked established, not glitzy or polished, but importantly it smelt fantastic. And he needed coffee. He wandered in and caught the eye of the elderly man behind the counter. Nico lifted his chin and the man nodded his own head towards a nearby table.

'*Caffè?*' he asked.

'*Si. Espresso. Per favore.*'

The man approached him with a perfectly made espresso with a thick crema on the surface.

'Your espresso,' the man said. 'Would you like something to eat?'

Nico did and asked to try a *pasticciotto*, a pastry filled with ricotta and custard.

When the man returned with the pastry he said, 'You're Niccolò Rossetti, aren't you?'

Nico was accustomed to being recognised in London, but hadn't expected to be recognised here.

'Do I know you?' Nico asked.

The man laughed. 'No, I know your show and your books. You're famous.'

'But not here, surely?'

'Why not? You are from Puglia.'

It took Nico a moment to let that sink in.

'There are not many famous chefs from Puglia. And even fewer from Tregua.'

Nico nodded. Emotions were swelling up inside him. It was strange to think of himself as well-known in the part of the world he had left as a ten-year-old.

'Are you here for a holiday?' the man asked.

'A research trip. My next book is going to be about Puglia. And my family,' he added.

The man nodded. 'That's wonderful. I'm sure your parents would be proud.'

Nico starred at the man, still searching for recognition. 'Did you know them?'

'Oh, no, but I do know why you left. And I remember the accident in which your father perished.'

Nico closed his eyes. He needed to get used to being reminded. He needed to not shut down each time it was mentioned. He felt the man's thick hand on his shoulder.

'I know that they would be proud. We are all proud.'

Nico opened his eyes and smiled at the man, then gestured for him to sit at the table. 'If you have a moment, I'd love to hear about this place.'

The man's face lit up. He introduced himself as Constanzo and he pulled out the nearest chair.

The two men spoke for ages about the business, how long he'd run it, where he got his produce. Nico learned that Constanzo's cousin owned the bakery that made the pastries, that business was slower in the down season but that they got a decent tourist trade in high season.

The whole encounter was so unexpected and pleasant and distracted Nico from his other concerns momentarily, until he realised he needed to leave.

'Do you mind if we stay in touch? We will be coming back in a few months to film and it would be great to see you again.'

'Of course! And next time bring *Bella* Freya.'

Nico froze.

The man knew Freya. Of course people knew her. She was nearly as famous as him. He told his audience about the dishes she loved the most, talked about her incessantly. She was the person behind his photos and behind the camera.

The person behind his success.

But if Freya returned to the States, the next time he travelled to Puglia he would be alone. Suddenly the delicious coffee and pastries were like lead in his stomach.

Nico said goodbye to Constanzo and strolled back through the streets. The sun was getting higher in the sky and he knew that he should get back to the hotel, but his feet dragged. His head ached and his limbs were like stone. Between the nightmare and everything else he hadn't managed to sleep much the night before. Every time he would come close to sleep his mind and body would turn back to Freya and the kiss.

Even when he managed to turn his brain to other things his body would have other ideas, and tingling excitement would rush through him. His limbs would ache with longing to hold her in them.

The last time they'd slept together the fallout had been catastrophic. Very nearly tragic. He couldn't let it happen again.

A buzzing sound distracted Freya from kissing Nico. Hooking her legs around his.

The buzzing was persistent. She tried to ignore it, as it felt so good rubbing her body against his. But the buzzing wouldn't stop.

She rolled over and suddenly Nico was gone and all that was left was her alarm. She fumbled around and pressed Snooze but lay there for a moment, trying to piece together the dream while she could still remember it. The feelings of fear, longing, excitement swirled together, unattached to actual events, but then the events began to come into focus, to slide into order.

She had been talking to Nico, in their living room at home. She told him she was thinking of moving back to California. She'd worn a new pink dress; one she'd purchased for that very conversation. Casual yet seductive. It had had the desired effect because when she'd asked him what she meant to him, he'd kissed her. Again and again.

And they had made love. Right there, on the sofa. And then in his room.

Except it wasn't a dream; this had happened. Suddenly it was all there. Her memories. Her past. Maybe not everything but most things. The important things. The most recent things.

The night before her birthday. The night before her accident. Her and Nico. Together.

Freya lay on her back, staring at the fan slowly spinning on the ceiling and doing nothing to cool her down. A thin sweat covered her skin and her heart raced.

She struggled to catch her breath.

Over an orgasm that had happened weeks ago. She shook and panted, even though she was only remembering it.

They had slept together. She'd known from the beginning that there was something between her and Nico and it hadn't all been in her imagination.

Why hadn't he told her? Was he trying to trick her?

No, that didn't fit.

He was so protective, so cautious. Even though he'd been the one to initiate the kiss last night, she hadn't just led him on; she'd practically dragged him into it.

He'd been the one to pull away. He'd been the one to refuse the invitation to her room. If he wanted to take advantage of her, he could have done so many times over.

Apart from the sex, there was something else he wasn't telling her, something that was buried in her lost memories or maybe something she'd never understood at all.

Her alarm buzzed again and she groaned. They were meant to be visiting an olive oil farm and factory. She needed to get up and dressed but was still out of breath. Her head was still whirling. She tried a few more memories, but only had glimpses of working in the restaurant. Of some of her colleagues. Of some faces and some names. Not everything, but so much more than she'd remembered yesterday. She got out of bed and went to the bathroom. She showered and under the hot steamy stimulation of the water more memories crept back, but still in disjointed fragments. Mostly of Nico.

Wrapped in a towel, she shuffled over to her suitcase and smiled at the clothes she'd packed, recognising them for the first time. These were not the clothes she'd planned on bringing, the ones she'd purchased for the trip, but old ones that had belonged to California Freya. Short denim skirts, tight T-shirts. Clothes she'd worn in Pasadena, but ones that she didn't wear in London.

Freya sat back onto the bed, suddenly more exhausted than ever.

The doctors were right; her memories hadn't all come back at once. She tried to remember helping him write the cookbook or taking the photos, but could only remember Nico. Him sitting next to her in their office, him asking her to taste a soup he'd made or some fresh focaccia. She couldn't remember designing the restaurant or their house, but somehow her memories of Nico and their relationship were coming into focus. How she'd loved him for so long. How she'd been so scared of losing his friendship if she told him how she felt. How she'd vowed to herself that more than anything it was important that they stay friends.

How he never seemed to catch on to her too-subtle hints. How he'd looked the night he'd opened his third restaurant, more delectable than any dish he'd served, dressed as he was in a crisp new suit. The sound of his laughter one time they'd sat in the Red Crown one night. She stared absent-mindedly out the window as these old memories played across her mind. One leading to another and then another. But like a film she hadn't finished watching, she didn't know the ending.

The memories were all somehow connected to Nico. He was the centre of her world and had been for so long, so it was only natural that now the essential memory of the night they had spent together had come back to her, others did too. She marvelled again at the strangeness and fickleness of the human brain.

Some memories were happy, some sad, but the thing she was most grateful to have slowly returning was the sense of confidence, certainty and grounding that had been missing for the past few weeks. She was good at her job; she was a great photographer. And a vibrant and energetic person. Jane and Lachlan? Those memories were still vague, yet she didn't want to dwell too long on retrieving them. Some things were best left forgotten.

The sound of a text message from Nico asking where she was alerted her to the time. Let him wait, she thought, but at the same time, she needed to see him, to see if he looked different to her than he had last night.

She dried herself off slowly, studied her face in the mirror and marvelled at the sense of familiarity. It wasn't a stranger looking back at her anymore. She knew this person. She knew who she was.

She was Freya McFadden. Photographer. Food stylist and publicist to Niccolò Rossetti.

Most importantly, she finally remembered her plan: if Nico wasn't prepared to give her what she wanted, she would leave London to find a man who was. A man who didn't have the same hang-ups as Nico, someone prepared to give her all the love she deserved.

It was with this newly remembered sense of certainty that she returned to the suitcase to decide what to wear. She moved items around, trying to find just the perfect outfit. Something that showed Nico exactly what he was missing out on. Her fingers brushed over the pink dress.

The dress she'd worn that night. She laughed.

Freya of a week ago had known this dress was special, even if she hadn't realised why.

She'd wear it. She had to. If only to see the look on his face.

She slipped it over her head, smoothed it down and looked at herself in the mirror. Freya of a month ago had paired it with stockings, boots and a jacket. But spring in Italy was perfect for wearing it on its own, with its cap sleeves, flattering bias cut and a neckline that was almost indecent. Because she was no longer going to play fair.

Freya drew in a deep breath, closed her eyes and let her new ability to access her memories revisit that night.

The night before her thirtieth birthday.

On her twenty-fifth birthday she'd been living in Pasadena, sacked from a job she hated, feeling as though the world was passing her by. On the eve of her thirtieth, her life was radically different; she had taken herself across the globe, forged a new life for herself, but a similar sense of stasis hung over her.

Her life was great, she loved working with Nico but something had changed in the past few months.

She'd realised she was in love with him.

Of course, any fool probably could have seen that long ago, but she hadn't. She had been so impressed and in awe of him when they'd first met and never imagined having a relationship with him. But as they'd gotten to know one another, become friends, things had changed. Freya had dated in London. She'd had a lot of first dates but never wanted to take things further. No one she'd met had ever quite matched up to Nico.

She had become very good at pushing aside the realisation that she loved Nico. It was too awkward. They were colleagues, flatmates and friends. And it was probably just a silly crush. And her life was great—she had a great job; she travelled the world. Her life was wonderful. Was she really going to give up all that by confessing that she loved him?

Maybe, she thought, as her birthday got closer, maybe she was. It was the eve of her next decade. And she had to do something.

So she'd bought the dress, set the scene, poured the wine and waited for him to arrive home.

She knew he was throwing a surprise party for her the next night. She hadn't let on that she knew but there wasn't much that happened in the restaurant she didn't know about. It was a lovely, thoughtful gesture and she suspected all her London friends would be there.

It would be the perfect time to say goodbye if everything went wrong with Nico. The perfect way to end her time in London.

Not that she wanted to leave, heavens no—she was hopeful that her declaration would have the opposite effect, but she had a plan B lined up just in case. A plane ticket to LAX.

Nico was cautious about relationships. He blamed himself for his parents' deaths but surely they could move past that together. There was so much they had done together in the past few years: opened two restaurants, launched his television career and written several books.

They'd overcome all sorts of obstacles with hard work, tenacity and sheer talent. They could build a romantic relationship too, as long as he felt the same way about her.

Freya had also bought a one-way plane ticket home. It was the superstitious part of her. So she couldn't chicken out at the last minute. She was going to tell him she loved him. Everything.

How she felt. What she wanted. What she needed.

And she was going to tell him that if he didn't feel the same, she had decided to go home to California.

She'd set the scene in their living room as best she could. Some white wine, and a big deep breath. He was sitting next to her, looking at his phone and choosing some music.

Before she could talk herself out of it or think twice, she said, 'Nico, I have to tell you something.'

He was singing away, putting on new music, and didn't turn. 'I know, Adele.'

'No, that's not it.'

'Not Ed Sheeran again? Okay, it is your birthday.'

'No, Nico, we need to talk.'

'Okay, Adele it is.'

He wasn't seeing her; he wasn't listening to her, even now. He never would. He'd never see her that way. He wasn't even listening to her properly now.

She took his phone from him and turned off the music.

'I need a change.'

He narrowed his yes, finally realising she wasn't talking about the music. 'What sort of change?'

'Maybe a change of job. A change of city.'

He tilted his head to one side, as though he didn't believe her. 'Two weeks ago, you told me you had the best job in the world.'

That had been true. They'd been in Cape Cod eating lobster next to the ocean. She had a job she loved and he was her best friend. Was she crazy to throw it all away?

No.

'It is, and I love it here, but I need more.'

'Puglia is coming up.'

'That's not what I mean.'

'Then what are you talking about?'

If she didn't tell him now, then she may never get this close again. She had to tell him how she felt or give up waiting for him.

'I can't keep going on like this.'

'Do you *have* another job?' He leaned forward and she smelt the last breath of his aftershave and the smell of the kitchen at the restaurant. Her body reeled with longing.

She shook her head.

'Then what?'

'I'm about to turn thirty.'

He grinned. 'I know that but…why does that mean you want to quit your job?'

Ordinarily it wouldn't. But when you were hopelessly in love with your boss it made it difficult to get on with your life.

'Because I need to make some decisions about my future.'

'And?'

'And…' Freya inched closer to him on the sofa. 'I need to know what I'm going to be to you in the future.'

Oh, dear. It was out there. There was no going back now. This wasn't quite how she'd imagined saying it; it wasn't poetic or persuasive, but the words rushed out of her in a large breath. She felt a moment of relief before a surge of panic while he processed her words.

'Do you ever think about us?' she whispered.

'Of course I do.'

'And?'

'And we work together. And live together. And you're my best friend.'

'I know, and it's wonderful and I'm probably crazy to put it all on the line, but I want more, Nico. And I want to know if you do too.'

'Of course I do.'

'You do?'

She couldn't breathe. It was so strange. It was

probably like being told you'd won the lottery. Disbelief.

'Freya, you are my person. I adore you. Of course I think about you. About us.'

Then he stopped talking.

'But?'

'I'm your boss.'

'I'll quit.'

He laughed. 'Freya, I'm not going to let you give up your career for me.'

I'd give up everything for you, she thought, but didn't say it.

Instead, she leaned towards him. Her hand was next to his and then his fingers brushed against hers. His face close, his eyes staring deep into hers, searching.

'I'm crazy about you,' she said.

They held each other's eyes, started falling into one another's gazes. She looked at his lips, subconsciously ran her tongue over her own. She'd waited so long for this moment and couldn't quite believe it might be about to happen.

Their faces were closer than ever and then his lips touched hers gently. Yet he didn't open his mouth and nor did she, waiting, longing, hardly able to breathe.

They held the moment, poised on the precipice. She let her declaration sink in a little further, waited as he steadied his breath, but it didn't steady. Instead it became as ragged as her heartbeat. Freya was light-headed by the time Nico finally began dragging his lips slowly across hers, the friction sending a wave of tiny sparks through her limbs. His lips explored hers as he ran his hand up her arm. Slowly but not hesitantly. They took the time to become accustomed to one another's taste and then without knowing how, her mouth was open and so was his and as the room began to swirl around her she fell back onto the sofa. Nico didn't take his mouth from hers, not for a moment. She ran her tongue slowly over his, exploring but most of all tasting the most sensuous dish they had ever shared.

'You are so beautiful,' he gasped through kisses, and her heart soared.

It was happening! If all your dreams came true, would you actually burst? It felt as though she might; desire and need were gathering and colliding in her in a mix that would have to find release or she would explode.

'You smell so good.' It was all she could manage to say, and a total understatement. He felt good. He felt amazing. His body on top of hers was the most wonderful thing she'd felt in her life and she would die happy, right here.

'You have no idea how many times I've thought about doing this,' he muttered into her neck.

'I think I have a pretty good idea.'

His hands slid under the hem of her dress, over her stockings, higher, and she moaned. She ran her hands over his back and lower, lower to his trousers and onto his bottom. He stilled at that point.

My hand is on my best friend's butt. And it feels as magnificent as it looks.

There was a moment when she feared they had reached the end of the line. The point where he would get off her and tell her it was all a mistake, but then she felt his moan in her neck and his lips on the swell of her breast and she was no longer afraid.

'I have a good idea,' she said.

'You have lots of them.'

'Yeah, but this is one of my best.'

'Does it have anything to do with us getting out of these clothes?'

'Great minds,' she said.

He unzipped her boots and dropped them onto the floor. She lifted his sweater over his head, and the shirt under quickly followed. He worked her stocking down with care and kisses and she did the same with his pants.

'Protection?' she asked.

'Upstairs.'

She groaned. She didn't think she could wait that long. It had been years.

'Later,' he said. 'Let's do this first.'

His fingers and lips explored her folds and knew exactly where to rub and the perfect pressure. The want inside her grew until it was almost overwhelming. She could hardly breathe as he kissed and stroked and caressed and licked and reached into places she hardly knew she had. Her heart pounded in her ears, a roar travelled through her body, his fingers and his mouth flew her into the air then placed her carefully back down to earth again.

'Wow,' she gushed.

'Wow is right.'

'We are such idiots.'

He laughed.

'We could have been doing this for years. Think of all the practice we could have had.'

'Practice? I think we're pretty good at it already.' His kisses trailed across her cheek and to the soft spot below her ear. She leaned her head back and released a moan. His laugh was hot against her neck.

'I don't want to lose you,' she said.

'You won't,' he replied.

Freya was sitting in the hotel lobby when Nico finally returned from his walk. She stood when he walked in and he stopped mid-stride. She was wearing the pink dress. That dress. The one that clung to her hips then swirled around her knees. The one with the neckline that he was helpless to drag his eyes up from. Though he tried his hardest as he walked towards her.

'Good morning, I hope you got back to sleep.'

A sly smile crept over her lips and dread gathered in his stomach again. 'I did. As it happens, I had a good sleep. With some interesting dreams.'

'Good, I'm sorry again that I woke you.'

'How many times have we slept together?' she replied.

Nico looked around. The clerk at the desk lifted his head but looked away when Nico caught his eye.

You knew this moment was coming.

'Can we go somewhere more private?' Nico asked.

'Tell me honestly. And don't even think about lying.'

'I'm not going to lie—I've tried not to lie.'

She let out a snort. 'Just tell me.' She stood with her feet apart and rooted herself to the spot.

Nico leaned in to whisper but in doing he became dangerously close to her. She smelt of roses and a warm shower, and worst of all, he could see straight down her dress to the lacy bra underneath. His traitorous body began to harden.

'It was just the one time.' And it was amazing. *The time that I will remember above all others, until the day I die. If I forgot every other time in my life, it would be alright as long as I remembered that night.* He hoped he could tell her all of that with just the expression in his eyes.

But her hands remained on her hips and she looked at him with one eyebrow raised.

'Okay, more than once, but just that one night.'

She nodded, as if in agreement. She'd remembered and guilt gripped at his stomach, almost making him double over. Her memories were returning. He should have been overjoyed and yet…

'Can we please go somewhere more private and talk?'

She nodded. 'Your room.'

He'd have preferred somewhere less intimate but was not about to argue. Once she'd heard what he was about to tell her she'd never want to be in his room again. Or in his life.

He followed her into the elevator and back to their rooms, trying not to notice the way her bottom looked under the fabric of the dress. Once in his room, he opened the door to the balcony off his room. It was fitting that the Adriatic Sea, the backdrop to all his failures, would bear witness to this conversation.

He didn't deserve her and he couldn't keep her safe.

'Why didn't you tell me or anyone that we were together?'

'Because…'

'*Were* we together?'

'It was new and we hadn't really talked about anything. And that's the truth.'

'But why didn't you tell me?'

'I wanted to, but you said you didn't want to know.' Even as he said it, he wanted to wince.

'I did say that, but I didn't mean *you.*'

'I couldn't tell you—you didn't *know* me. You had no memory of me at all. It would have been too confronting. You needed to remember for yourself.'

Freya stepped back and hugged herself, despite the warmth of the day.

'Later. You could have told me later. You could have told me when I asked about what kind of relationship we had.'

'I've thought about telling you every day, but it was just that one time.'

She rolled her eyes, as well she might. The fact that it was one night didn't make what he had done forgivable.

'The night before my birthday. The night before the accident.'

'Yes.'

'But you *didn't* tell me.'

'I didn't want to hurt you or confuse you. I didn't know what to do. I struggled with this decision every day.' He rubbed his face with his hands. 'I tried to convince you that we were friends, you didn't even believe that. Besides, I didn't see what the point of telling you would be.'

She threw her head back and groaned. 'Because I'd know. I'd understand.'

He shook his head.

She turned from him and looked around the room. 'I'm not saying it was the right thing. Just the least-worst thing,' he said. There were so many things he should have done differently.

'It might have been confronting but it would've been the truth.'

'I'm sorry. Truly. I… I didn't know what to do. Above all else, I was trying to protect you.'

'Protect me from what?'

Now she knew about their night together, he had to tell her everything. Then maybe she'd understand why he'd struggled so much with this secret. That all he'd ever wanted to do was to protect her.

'How much do you remember?' he asked.

'Not everything. But I remember a lot more than I did yesterday, and more every minute. I remember I told you I was thinking of leaving London and I asked you how you felt about me. And we kissed. In our living room.'

'And do you remember what happened after that?' he asked.

He remembered. He thought about it every hour of his life. The sofa, their limbs, knowing there were more comfortable places to be doing it, but also knowing that they had already wasted so much time. Knowing that neither of them wanted to wait a moment longer.

'Do you remember the day of the accident?'

She shook her head. 'Nothing. But Dr Jamal said that memory may never come back.'

Nico dragged his hand over his face again. Her

remembering the night they had spent together was not the worst thing. That was not the thing he dreaded telling her.

'Tell me about the accident,' she began. 'I know it wasn't your fault. The police told me that. And the doctors.'

This was where he was meant to fill in the blanks for her. Tell her what had been happening when the lorry had failed to give way and smashed into them. When he had failed to notice and swerve.

'Are you going to tell me or are there more secrets?' she said.

He hated to tell another lie but what choice did he have? 'We were just talking.'

She cocked her head to one side. 'What were we talking about?'

He could lie. Or tell her he didn't remember either. He had been knocked around in the accident too. Nothing like Freya but the shock and grief he'd felt after the accident had been all too real. The sleepless nights he'd been experiencing since. The nightmares. He drew a deep breath. He simply had to do the least-worst thing.

'Your hand was on my knee.'

All the colour left her face. 'Are you saying it was my fault?'

'No! Not at all. I turned to look at you.' *And my heart swelled and I wanted to reach for you. I couldn't take my eyes off you, couldn't believe how lucky I was. And I spoke to you and then the truck hit.*

'I was looking at you and I wasn't paying attention to the road and I didn't see the truck.' That was the truth. At least most of it.

'But you had right of way.'

'I should've been able to avoid the accident. I should've been able to see it coming.'

Freya looked into the distance.

He wasn't prepared for what she said next.

'So, we were together.'

'Yes, we were in the car.'

'No, I mean we had sex, and then we were together in the car.'

'Yes.'

'So, were we in a relationship? *Are* we in a relationship?'

'No.'

'Did we break up?'

'No, but—'

'It was a one-night stand?'

'No, but Freya—'

'You regret sleeping with me.'

'I wouldn't say it like that.'

'Then how would you say it?'

Her words cut him more perfectly than the finest sous chef could manage. She was so angry. And understandably so.

'We made love, and it was wonderful, but I

don't think it should happen again. I don't think we should have a relationship.'

'Why?' Her tone was laced with anger and hurt, but most of all bafflement. 'I was there that night. Parts of my memory might still be returning but that night I remember with perfect clarity. In a million megapixels. The memory of it woke me up this morning.'

Nico grasped the rail on the balcony. He couldn't look at her. He couldn't face himself.

'Because I hurt you. I never wanted to hurt you.'

'Then you shouldn't have slept with me.'

'No, I meant the accident.'

'It wasn't your fault.'

'But it was. I was driving and I couldn't keep you safe. Don't you see?'

'All I see is that you thought you had gotten away with sleeping with me. Amnesia, how convenient.'

'No, Freya, please. I couldn't save my father. I couldn't save my mother. And the moment our relationship changed I almost lost you too.'

'I don't get it. Is it the amnesia, or is this just not right? Help me.'

'You're my best friend and I care for you and I don't want to lose you.'

'But you just don't want the commitment or the responsibility of a full, loving, committed relationship.'

He closed his eyes tight with frustration. That wasn't it at all.

Except…

'I don't know how much you remember about everything, about me, about before.'

She shrugged. The doctors had told them both that her memories would come back in pieces, that even when she thought she remembered her past that there still might be gaps.

'When I was five, I stood on a dock, just down the coast from here, and watched as my father's fishing boat capsized and sank. I watched as he waved for help and I couldn't do anything. By the time help arrived, it was too late. That was my fault.'

'Nico, no.'

'No. Please listen. When he died, they told me I had to look after my mother. I tried and tried and I did my best, but when I was ten, she died of a broken heart. I couldn't stop that either.'

Freya bit her bottom lip and was looking like she was going to argue but mercifully let him say the next thing.

'And a few weeks ago, I slept with my best friend. And it was so wonderful and so distracting, I forgot for a moment that I can't look after people. But I was driving her to her birthday lunch and I was too busy looking at her and marvelling at how beautiful she is that I wasn't paying attention and the next thing I knew we were cleaned up by a lorry and I was standing there watching her being cut lifeless from the car.'

'Nico—'

'And I thought you were dead. I thought I'd killed you. And we didn't know for days if you would ever wake up, and then we waited some more to see if you would. And then when you did you didn't remember me at all and as much as that hurt, it was also a blessing because if you didn't remember me then I couldn't hurt you anymore.'

His mind seemed to leave his body as he said the next words. It was the only way to get them out. It was the next-to-last thing in the world he wanted, yet the last thing was still so much worse. 'You were right all along—it would be best if you went home to California. Trust me, you'll be better off that way.'

CHAPTER EIGHT

FREYA NODDED, STOOD AND smoothed down her dress.

'I assume you still want to go out today?'

'You don't have to come,' he said.

'Of course I will. It's my job. It's why I came here in the first place.'

'Freya, really.'

'No, I came to work and I'll work,' she said calmly, and was shocked to realise it wasn't an act. She was calm.

Or numb with shock.

There was a fine line between the two.

He cared for her, but felt too guilty about his parents' deaths to have a relationship with her. From anyone else that would sound like a bad excuse, but Nico was her friend and she wanted to give him the benefit of the doubt and believe it was more complicated than that. Even though he hadn't told her everything about their relationship, she didn't believe he'd done it maliciously or to manipulate her. She could see the conflict behind his eyes.

She hadn't fully processed what Nico had just told her and wasn't sure if she ever would but an instinct kicked in. Self-preservation. What he'd just told her had been too momentous to process, let alone overcome. Together with all the revelations of the past few hours she needed time, space and energy. She couldn't deal with it all now and she was damned if she was going to fall apart. At least not yet.

They had things to do.

'I'll meet you downstairs in fifteen minutes.'

Nico's jaw dropped and she smiled to herself. He didn't expect she would be up for the trip, but the fact that she was meant he had to be as well.

You can suffer through this with me.

She'd come here for work and they were going to work and she wasn't going to let this or anything stop her from doing so. Whether she was just repressing everything that had happened this morning or in the past few weeks she neither knew nor cared. She was going to do her job.

Freya gathered her things, brushed her hair and prepared to face the day. She picked up the keys for their rental car and considered them. Now it made sense that he wanted her to drive. She was accustomed to driving on the right side of the road, but Nico was a good driver. She remembered that much. And she doubted Dr Jamal would have recommended a recovering amnesiac be in charge of a car. And yet, here she was. She tossed the keys into the air and caught them with a sigh.

Out of Monopoli they drove over rolling green hills, along narrow roads lined with dry stone walls. Freya opened all the windows to the car and let the sweet spring breeze blow over them. Their first spot was an ancient olive grove and the adjacent factory, where they met the proprietors of the boutique specialty olive oil. The olive mush was dried out and then used as a dry fuel and organic fertiliser.

'I always wondered what they did with the rest of the olive bits once they squeeze out the oil and now I know!' she said to Nico, glimpsing a small smile cross his face.

The next stop was at a fortress garden, a medieval garden that had been fortified to protect it from the waves of invading forces that had occupied Puglia over the centuries. Much of the castle was in ruins but the garden was still flourishing and produced all manner of vegetables, flowers and herbs, including very old varietals.

All day she remembered how much she loved her job, how wonderful it was that she got to sightsee and eat for a living.

No other job will be as good as this one.

Maybe not, but she wanted more in her life. She

wanted love. Not simply friendship, but passion. And if Nico wasn't the person to give it to her, she needed to move on. It was hard—it would be hard—but it would be more difficult in the long run to stay.

'Are you sure you don't want to drive?' she asked when they returned to the car.

'Are you not feeling well?'

She thought about lying, of forcing him to get into the driver's seat, but realised that wouldn't solve anything.

'I'm fine.'

'You're more comfortable driving on the right than I am.'

She stifled a snort.

Nico didn't want to deal with his guilt. It was so overpowering, so ingrained, and he maybe didn't have the capacity to. For the first time she not only remembered Nico's unwillingness to begin a relationship but understood it. His claim that he couldn't be in a relationship wasn't simply an excuse; it was a deep-seated fear, one that she hadn't been able to shift, not after five years of closeness. And after everything that had happened in the past few weeks, she now understood she had no chance. Nico would only ever be her friend. If she wanted marriage and a family, if she wanted that sort of life, she had to untangle herself from him—both her life and her emotions. Because she couldn't love anyone else while she lived and worked for him.

Somewhere on the road back to Monopoli, with a lump deep in her chest, it was settled.

Freya would return to the States. Maybe she'd try New York. San Francisco. Chicago. Going back to greater LA seemed like a backward step after the past five years. A new city would be full of new challenges and best of all, no memories.

That's what she needed, a clean slate.

New place, new people.

She wished she could share this thought with Nico but it was far better not to. He was focusing on the map and giving her directions.

She didn't hate him. For the first time all day she understood him. Understood why he hadn't told her everything that had happened between them. He couldn't change who he was and nor could she. It was sad, but acceptance settled down on her.

She would have to leave London.

They had a booking at a nearby trattoria for dinner. Just the one meal as they'd been grazing on food all afternoon. He ordered a glass of local wine and she ordered a cocktail.

They tried each other's drinks and meals as a matter of course, and the friendliness of the gesture hit her for the first time.

We've been sharing drinks and meals for years.

It was the best way to try as many dishes as possible. And a surefire way to increase intimacy.

And they did it again now.

Her brain may have accepted that she would be leaving him, but her body had other ideas. Each time their hands brushed, her heart raced and her skin buzzed.

She had to leave London. And Nico.

But not just yet. They still had a few more days.

Across the table from her, Nico ate his meal, his lids low over his dark eyes he was so consumed by enjoyment of the taste. She shivered. What was it like to make love with him? Her memory of that night was patchy, incomplete. She remembered feeling nervous, exhilarated, but not the look on his face or the sounds he made. Could she? Could they? Just one more time? Could they make love one more time when her memories would not be clouded by amnesia? One more time to remember him by?

Freya was only half paying attention as Nico discussed the notes he had taken from the day, the recipes he'd like to cook, places to return to.

'We should go back the olive oil farm when we come to shoot,' he said.

'You should,' she corrected. She saw the confusion cross his face and the moment of realisation.

Life was about remembering the bad things, over and over, she thought.

'Yes,' he said and coughed.

I don't have to go! she wanted to scream. *You're the one sending me away!* She rubbed her temple; her head was sore from stress and tiredness.

If they could make love just one more time, so they both remembered, she could have an intact memory to take with her into the future. Being with her one more time might make him remember all the reasons why he didn't want her to leave.

She lowered her head. No. That was a fantasy. Unhelpful thinking. Nico had made his mind up. It was a mutual decision; he couldn't give her the type of relationship she wanted, and she'd decided she needed to leave.

'New York it is,' she muttered.

'New York?'

'Sorry, yes, I was thinking aloud.'

'You're going to New York?'

'It's just an idea. I don't know about LA. It seems like a backward step. New York would be a bigger adventure.'

He nodded but looked away.

'I had an offer from a place there last year, didn't I?'

Nico's eyes darkened.

'Do you not want me to talk about it? I'll stop, but I'd appreciate your advice.'

'It's fine,' he grunted, though he was clearly anything but.

Pain gripped her temples like a vice. She took a sip of water but it was no match for the agony that was closing in on her. She closed her eyes and put her head in her hands but the pain began to spread. She hadn't had a migraine like this since she'd been in the hospital.

'Are you okay?' She sensed, rather than saw, Nico lean across the table.

'I'm tired. I need to rest.'

'We'll go. Wait here while I pay.'

His voice was rough, quick, but the command was unnecessary. Her vision was blurred by the pain spreading under her skull. She took deep breaths and drank some water but the pain didn't subside. So much for managing to cope with all the stress she'd been under in the past day.

Nico returned to the table, took her by the elbow and led her out of the restaurant. He hailed a cab and helped her into it. 'I could have walked,' she said.

'No way, Freya. You're unwell. I've pushed you too hard.'

She hated being coddled, particularly as she'd made more progress today than in the past three weeks combined, but with the vice tightening around her skull she lacked the capacity to argue. Back at the hotel he guided her into the lobby and up to their rooms. He swiped into his room and led her through the adjoining door to hers. She kicked off her shoes and fell on her bed. She sensed the room getting quiet and darker; Nico must have closed all the blinds and curtains.

The next thing she was aware of was Nico sitting gently down on the side of her bed. 'I've got you some pain medication. Do you think you can sit up to take it?'

She rolled herself over and pushed herself up. The disorientation wasn't as bad if she kept her eyes closed. She took the tablets he offered her.

'I don't want to leave you alone.'

'It's just a migraine. I've had them before.'

'Yes, but not three weeks after a coma. Not the day you get a whole lot of memories back. I knew it was a mistake to bring you here.'

She wanted to tell him there was no way he was going to stop her, that coming here, however unsettling, had still helped her. But all she could do was groan and lie back down.

'Need to sleep.'

She felt him get off the bed and step away.

He was gone. It was painful, yet also a relief. When he was around her, she couldn't think straight. She had wild ideas of trying to seduce him. Of ignoring the inevitable. As much as she wanted him to lie down next to her and pull her to him, she still knew how risky it would be.

She pulled the spare pillow close to her chest instead, took some deep breaths and in moments she was asleep.

The sound of a someone clearing their throat awakened him. Nico straightened up in the chair and as he did, he felt a strain in his neck and winced.

Freya was sitting up in her bed. The curtains were still drawn but the brightness of the sunlight creeping around their edges let him know the morning was well underway.

'Please tell me you didn't sleep there?' she said.

He grunted. 'I wouldn't call it sleep, exactly.' He'd sat in the armchair googling 'coma,' 'amnesia' and 'migraine'. Some sites had been reassuring. Others had told him to take her to hospital immediately. Eventually he'd messaged Dr Jamal, who had thankfully called him right back and reassured him that as long as she was comfortable and coherent that she would be fine but as soon as she had difficulty walking or speaking, he was to take her hospital right away. Nico's body flowed with relief to see her sitting up, looking bright and speaking normally.

'You were there all night?'

'Of course.'

'Of course nothing. I told you I was okay.'

'You weren't. I was worried about you.'

'I'm fine.' She spun her legs over the side of the bed, still wearing the pink dress. He watched her stand and his mouth went dry.

'Will you be alright if I go and have a shower?' he asked.

She laughed. 'I'm fine. I'm going to have a shower too. By myself.'

They looked at one another. He was about to tell her to be careful again but the glare she gave him warned him not to.

She didn't want his concern, and maybe that was what he deserved. He'd been the one to get her into this mess.

'I'm still allowed to worry about you,' he mumbled to himself.

'Pardon?'

He shook his head. He didn't want to argue, but he knew he had little right to play the concerned-lover card. At best he was her friend, at worst, her boss. He'd slept with her, nearly killed her and yesterday had told her that it had all been a mistake, that they did not have a future together. It was understandable she didn't want him looking after her.

Yet, he couldn't help saying, 'I think you should take it easy today.'

'I'm great, really. The migraine is gone, my head feels much clearer. I just need some coffee. Something small to eat.'

They both showered and when he knocked again on her door, she called him to come in. She'd ordered breakfast to be delivered to her room and was sitting on the balcony with a mug of coffee in her hands.

Without meaning to, he let out a sigh, a deep half groan from the centre of his very being.

'What?' Freya looked startled.

'Sorry. I'm just tired.'

It wasn't a lie. He hadn't got much sleep last night. But he wasn't sighing about that.

He was sighing because Freya was wearing a skimpy halter top and short denim shorts. Her long legs were stretched out onto the chair next to hers. Her dark blonde hair was tidied up loosely on the top of her head and he could see every inch of her gorgeous smooth skin soaking in the morning sun.

She was beautiful.

She always looked beautiful, but seeing her sitting like this now was like a punch in his gut.

'Do you want some coffee?'

An intravenous drip of the stuff, he thought, but said, 'Thanks,' and pulled up the spare chair.

'So, I guess I should help you find my replacement.'

It felt as though someone had poured concrete down his throat.

'I can do that,' he mumbled.

'I can help, is what I'm trying to say.'

'There's no need.'

He was blunt, but he had to be. How else could he be? His best friend was leaving. Forever. He didn't want to think about it. He couldn't think about it. He might move on from the denial stage at some point but not yet.

She turned to him and put her hands on her hips. 'What's up?'

'Do you really have to ask?'

'You want me to leave. You told me to.'

'I know, but I'm not overjoyed by the idea.'

'Then?'

'We both know it's for the best. It's what you wanted, remember?'

She flinched. *Remember* was a word he should strike from his vocabulary.

'We talked about it. Before and yesterday. You'll be happier back in the States. I support your decision.'

'Except for the groaning.'

'I wasn't…'

Freya raised her eyebrow.

'Look, we just have a few more days left here. Can we think about the future when we get back?' he asked.

Freya twisted her mouth. He knew the expression. It meant, *Okay, I'll humour you for now but this isn't over.*

He didn't need her to say it aloud. He knew this was all far from over.

CHAPTER NINE

THEIR ITINERARY HAD them spending the day in Monopoli, which was just as well. He didn't want Freya to drive after her migraine and he certainly didn't want to drive her anywhere. They wandered around the narrow streets of Monopoli's old quarter and explored shops, markets and cafes. They visited the picturesque harbour, surrounded on three sides by ancient stone walls and embankments. Freya chatted happily as they went, pointing to things she saw but also remarking on random things she'd done in the past as her memories gradually came back to her. His heart swelled at the sight of her face, delighting in the memories of the past few years. Memories of their time together. He didn't think it was possible feel such relief; Freya was back.

She was also recovered from her migraine. Happy. Laughing. And surely the flirtatious looks she was giving him were all in his mind. *What about the wink she gave you when you were looking at the vegetable market?* An involuntary twitch? Almost definitely.

The idea of making this next television series without her was incomprehensible.

So he wasn't going to think about it.

Not yet.

Maybe he could convince her to stay. Help her get a place of her own in London, put a little distance between them, but at least not lose her across an ocean. But even the thought of Freya living somewhere that wasn't their house also twisted his stomach into all sorts of uncomfortable knots. The thought of her living with someone else… Being with someone else…

So he wouldn't think about that either.

But while he was doing his best to convince his brain not to think about her, his body had other ideas. His heart beat rapidly anytime they came within inches of one another, anytime he breathed in her scent. His limbs tingled and his stupid muscles tensed and jerked in all kinds of unfortunate ways.

They returned to their hotel after lunch for a rest to avoid the afternoon heat. He was looking forward to putting a small amount of space between them and having a break from the way his pulse quickened each time he accidentally brushed his arm against Freya's or when she smiled at him knowingly. Suggestively.

'See you in a bit,' he said at the door to his

room. If he could only have an hour or two alone, but somewhere where he knew she was safe, then he'd be able to sort out his head and think sensibly again.

'Yes.' Freya turned to her door but then spun back around. 'You don't want a relationship. For reasons I don't fully agree with but that's beside the point—they're your reasons. And I'm going back to the States, so I don't think starting a relationship is a good idea either.'

'What are you saying?' *Please don't be going where I think you're going. Not now. I don't think I have the energy to resist you.*

'I'm saying we like having sex. We're clearly good at it. We may as well give it another go.'

He laughed, but it was driven by nerves, not amusement. 'You say it like it's easy.'

'Isn't it? I don't recall you having any difficulties in the past.'

That did it. The heat in his chest went from slow flame to forest fire in an instant.

She stepped towards him and he filled his lungs with her, loving the way the breath carrying her scent filled up his body. Ordinary air was nothing after breathing in the air she inhabited.

Freya moved closer, brushing her body against his. Her halter neck showed the smooth skin of her shoulders and chest. Delicious, lickable skin.

'Freya, you're not making this easy.'

'It's not meant to be easy.' She slipped her soft

hand into his and drew her fingers in and out of his. The friction between their fingers shouldn't have felt as indecent as his body thought it did.

'But should it be this hard?' The air dragged painfully over his throat.

'Probably. Because we care for each other. No matter what else is going on, we still like one another.'

Against all reason, Nico closed his eyes and dipped his face closer to her neck. He felt her breathe in as well, felt her hand tighten around his. With her free hand she grasped his waist and pressed herself against him. She shivered and he realised his lips were tracing their way lazily from her throat up her neck and to her face.

Her hips were pliant and strong against his and he shifted back and forth to enjoy the full effect. He groaned.

'Are you sure?' he whispered, unable to make more of a sound.

'I wouldn't want us to miss this last chance.'

'Freya…' He couldn't. Not again. Because if they did this again, he didn't trust himself to be able to say goodbye.

'For old times.'

'It was one night.'

'And three times.'

She remembered. She remembered it all. There was no point hiding anything from her, or from himself. They had made love. Glorious, amazing, powerful love.

'Freya, you know as well as I do that this isn't a good idea.'

She raised one perfect eyebrow. 'I didn't realise how much you like to play hard to get.'

He grunted. 'I don't like it one little bit. I hate that I can't resist you.'

'*Hate*'s a strong word.'

But what he felt for her was just as strong.

'You're very persuasive,' he said.

'You don't have to resist.'

'You know I do.'

He had to protect her. This was risky, outright dangerous. She'd realise that one day. But right now, it was too late. The train had left the station. It had nearly left the tracks entirely. He moaned. Every last scrap of his inhibitions was destroyed by the tidal wave of desire that was surging through him. Her breath on his skin, her hot lips on his, her own moans reverberating through him.

She tugged his hand towards her room and he was powerless to pull away. She opened the door to her room and it closed behind them with a click.

'If not for old times, then for goodbye?' he said. For the last time.

'Just one more time for the sake of my memories,' she pleaded.

He couldn't argue with that, but he couldn't

argue at all. He couldn't speak. It was all he could do to breathe. He longed for his mind to take a picture-perfect memory of this moment. Of the sensation of her fingers sliding under his waistband. Of her lips on his hipbone as she eased his pants off him. Of the taste of her breasts as he kissed her until she cried out. Of all of it. Of each sound, each smell, each caress, hard, sweet, soft and even the bitter pain. All of it. To preserve all of it in his memories and mind forever. And ever.

His head spun, his body pounded, and they moved until they were both lost.

I want to do this for the rest of my life.

It was amazing. More amazing than he'd ever allowed himself to remember. He was flying, dancing, everything… Swirling and falling with her. His best friend. His Freya.

They landed, body and soul, and as his breath returned so did his senses.

What had he done? He looked down at her; her eyes were closed but the look of bliss on her face was unmistakable.

And terrifying.

This was most definitely not the plan.

He'd promised himself he wouldn't do this. Not again.

He was a cad to the hundredth degree.

Freya lay facedown on her bed, panting, body spent, head whirling. Nico lay sprawled next to her, also panting, his arm resting unconsciously across her back.

'That was even better than I remember,' she muttered into the pillow.

If that was their one last time then it was worth it.

And yet it wasn't.

What a stupid idea to think that one last time would be a harmless way of saying goodbye.

How could she *ever* have forgotten how it was to be with him?

'What was that?' he murmured. His voice deep and rough and never sexier.

'Mmm,' she replied. Hardly her most articulate answer but all she wanted to say to him at that point. She was even dreading sitting up and looking him in the face, afraid her eyes, her entire expression would expose her true feelings.

That was amazing. Let's do it again. Immediately.

But they couldn't. That wasn't the deal. One time was meant to be enough. One time was meant to be the end.

Except now they had done it, the memory may as well have been tattooed across her brain. Making love to Niccolò Rossetti was the best thing she had ever done in her life.

And it was over.

Maybe some things were better left forgotten.

'Are you okay?' he asked, rolling over.

'Never better.' It was both the truth and an outright lie. 'You?'

'Oh, Freya,' he sighed and she knew that was as much of an answer he was going to give her.

He may have enjoyed it as much as she had but it was different for him. He wasn't even contemplating taking their relationship to a different level. He never had been. For him it wasn't about saying goodbye, but about satisfying her. Almost like a favour.

You practically begged him.

The bubbles of bliss floating through her were washed away by a wave of shame.

You feel far more for him than he does for you. That's never going to change.

You won't be the one to change him. You're just Freya McFadden, who lacks the right energy. Who isn't vibrant enough.

She felt pressure building behind her nose and eyes and jumped out of bed.

'I'm just going to have a quick shower before dinner,' she said and rushed to her bathroom before the tears had a chance to flow.

She pulled herself together in the shower.

Work. Concentrate on the work.

It was what she'd always done. Five years of sexual tension had been tempered by good ol'-fashioned honest hard work.

So that was what they would do now. Go out, drink, eat and pretend that it was hard work and that sharing wine and gourmet food on the Adriatic coast didn't resemble a very romantic evening.

There would be no time to think about the afternoon, about damp sheets, the cool sea breeze brushing over their naked skin. No time to remember how it felt to move on top of him or the way his face melted with desire.

No time at all.

Except for when they were walking down one of Monopoli's narrow cobblestone lanes. Or waiting for their food to arrive. Or taking a sip of her spritz.

Or pretty much every moment of the evening.

Their conversation was stilted, which didn't help to keep her mind off what they had spent the afternoon doing. They had made love. It had been wonderful—she'd never felt closer to him—so why were they both struggling so much now? To carry on even a basic conversation? Why was he not even meeting her eyes?

The food was wonderful, everything she had imagined it would be. Worse yet, her work brain was beginning to engage and before she'd even realised what she was doing she was thinking of ways to display the food, how to photograph it, the background colours, the themes she would use to show it all off to its best advantage.

You won't photograph this food or this city. Or this place.

Her chest clenched and she pushed all her feelings down. Despite wanting to sleep with Nico more than anything else in her life, she was now beginning to wonder whether her mind had erased the memory of the night before her birthday for a good reason. It was possible to want to remember something so much and also need to forget about it completely at the same time.

Their conversation over dinner was awkward even though they had the meal to provide some topics of discussion, but it was practically nonexistent on the walk back to the hotel. When they reached their room doors and Nico said, 'Do you want to come into my room?' Freya was momentarily lost for words.

Her stomach was full, her limbs loose from the wine. Her body wanted to reach for him, pull him to her. To lose herself in him again. And again.

But it wouldn't be again and again. It would just be one more time. Or maybe two. And that wasn't enough.

You're not enough. That's what it comes down to. Not vibrant enough. Not the right energy.

'Nico, it was one last time. I promised.'

'I promised too,' he said and a shy smile crept over his lips.

She stood on her toes and pressed a quick kiss to his rough cheek.

'Good night. See you in the morning.'

She locked the door to her room before she could change her mind.

If closing the door on her hotel room was that hard, how could she possibly manage to close the door on their entire life together?

CHAPTER TEN

SHE SLEPT POORLY, but she still slept. This was their last day in Monopoli and Tregua. Tomorrow they would drive across Italy's ankle to Taranto and the parts of Puglia neither of them had been before.

New places. No memories. A clean slate. They couldn't get there fast enough as far as Freya was concerned, but first Nico had to make one last visit to Tregua and Anna.

Until he returned in a few months' time.

But today would be Freya's last trip. She would have to take many notes and photographs to hand over to Nico and whoever it was who replaced her.

Work. Concentrate on the work.

'Do you want to drive?' she asked, not to goad him but in the genuine hope that after last night something might have shifted inside him. That he might be less afraid. That he might be brave enough to get behind the wheel with her sitting next to him.

But he shook his head. 'I'm better at navigating.'

'You're not, you know,' she muttered quietly enough that he only gave her a puzzled look.

Like last time, she drove until the lanes became too narrow for her to drive comfortably down and parked the car. They didn't have far to walk; Tregua was small. Small and unspoilt. It didn't have the tourist numbers that Bari or Monopoli had, though the village was no less beautiful. Perhaps more so because of its authentic, unspoilt nature. She drank it all in, tried to commit it as best she could to her faulty memory. This would be the last time she came here. Because in a few days she'd say goodbye to Nico forever.

Nothing had really changed in the last month. She'd known deep down all along that she wasn't enough for Nico, that she would never be enough to shift whatever it was inside him that was holding him back. Nico was never going to love her as she loved him. The feeling twisted inside her, threatened to overwhelm her but she talked it back down. *You will be okay; you will move on. You will find someone who sees how special you are.*

But when they arrived at Anna's and she welcomed Freya in, Freya found she couldn't step over the threshold. She no longer belonged to this part of Nico's life.

'Why don't I give you both a moment?' Freya said.

Nico and Anna protested that it wasn't necessary.

'I know, but I'd like to take some photographs,

for the person who takes over from me.' She noticed Anna give Nico a puzzled look but she didn't care.

Let him tell her I'm leaving, she thought. *I don't think I can.*

As soon as Freya left, Anna rounded on him.

'What did she mean?'

'Freya's moving back to the States.'

Anna shook her head. 'Why on earth would she do that?'

'She wants to start the next stage of her life.' *And I can't be the man she wants. She deserves more than I can give her.*

Anna frowned. 'But her life is in London. With you.'

'I can't give her the life she wants.'

Anna laughed. 'The pair of you! You have a beautiful life. Sure, you live in rainy London, not beautiful Puglia, but I see the pair of you. You have a wonderful business, a great friendship.'

'It's complicated.'

'What's complicated? You just tell her. Even I can say "I love you" in English.'

I love you. Was it that obvious?

'I have told her,' he said.

Anna's face brightened with delight but then her shoulders fell.

'And she didn't say it back?'

'No, she did.' *And moments later the lorry hit*

us and the next thing I knew they were cutting her from the car.

'And she doesn't remember?' Anna guessed.

'No, she doesn't. She remembers most other things, but not that.'

Dr Jamal had always told them both that patients such as Freya often didn't regain memory of the accident or the time immediately before it. And he couldn't tell her this. Not now. Not when saying it in the first place had nearly killed her.

'So you just tell her again! Simple.'

'No, I can't.'

'You said it once. You just say it again. So she remembers, so she knows. Niccolò, it's deceitful not to tell her.'

'I'm not lying. I'm protecting her.'

'Protecting her from what?'

From me. 'Telling her won't do any good.'

'Phfft,' Anna said. Disagreement sounded the same in every language. 'She deserves your honesty.'

'She also deserves to have a long and happy life and I can't give her that.'

Anna screwed up her face.

'It's for the best,' he pleaded.

'The best for who?'

'For her.'

'Rubbish, she loves you.'

'As a friend.'

Anna laughed. 'Is that what you think? I thought you were smarter than that.'

Nico shook his head. Freya loved him as a friend. Even as a lover. And maybe she even thought they could be something more but that would pass. It was natural she saw him as a life partner, a husband, the father of her children, because they were so close. But she was worried about turning thirty. Assessing her life. Thinking of the future. So it was natural her gaze fell to him, given that they were so close. But when she moved away, she'd realise that he couldn't give her everything she needed. That he couldn't keep her safe.

So he had to let her go, to find someone who would love her completely, unconditionally, forever. Someone who could protect her.

'I can't hurt her.'

'But if you let her go, aren't you doing just that?'

No. He'd be saving her. 'I need to protect her.'

'Oh, you silly macho man. Where did that idea come from? You must protect each other and the best way to do that is living on the same continent to begin with.'

'I couldn't look after my mother,' he said. Anna knew the truth; she'd understand *this*.

'What do you mean?'

'After my father, she died. I wasn't enough for her.'

'I don't understand what you're saying.' She took his hand in hers but didn't laugh.

'It isn't just that, though. I couldn't look after Mama.'

'You did look after her.'

'Then why wasn't she happy? Why did she die?'

'Her heart gave out.'

'Exactly. She died of a broken heart.'

'Well, that's just a saying. She had several heart attacks.'

'At forty-eight?'

'Yes.'

'That's too young.'

'It happens. Especially with diabetes.'

'What?'

'Diabetes. *Diabete*,' Anna said it in English and then Italian.

Nico leaned forward. It sounded the same in Italian as it did in English.

'Your aunt never told you?' Anna asked.

He shook his head. 'No.'

'Maybe she assumed you knew. Your mother had many underlying issues, which I suppose she kept from you. You were so very young.'

'I was ten.' He remembered everything!

'Yes, which is young to understand that your mother has debilitating health concerns. We always thought she had more time.'

He remembered his mother wasn't always well,

was often tired, but he never connected that to her heart failure.

'None of it was your fault. But if you take anything away from this, get yourself a good cardiologist now and watch your cholesterol. You have those genes too.'

'They told me she died of a broken heart.'

'That's just a saying,' Anna repeated and held up her hands. 'It's what people say to show that she loved your father very much. But losing him didn't kill her. Losing him made her cling even more strongly to life because she had to look after you. She never wanted to die. She never wanted to leave you. She loved you so much.'

Anna got up to make them both a coffee. Nico insisted he do it, but he didn't feel the joy he thought he would pottering around this kitchen from his childhood.

A medical explanation was all well and good, but he knew the truth; losing his father had destroyed his mother. There was more than one way to die of grief. If his father had lived, his mother would have as well. Nico was certain of it.

Freya arrived back at Anna's, her face bright and clearly invigorated by what she had seen.

Maybe she'll decide to stay after all?

It was a vain hope. He didn't want her to leave, but he knew she wanted more from her life than he could give her. Marriage. Children. Things she would be amazing at. The life she should have.

But not with you.

'Are you heading straight back to Monopoli?' Anna asked.

'Yes, but I thought we'd go lay some flowers for Papa at the harbour first.'

'Why there?' Anna asked.

'Because that's where the accident was. Where the boat sank.'

Anna shook her head vigorously. 'No, it's not. The accident was off the point. Way off.'

'No, it was at the harbour. I saw it.'

Anna laughed. 'You didn't see it. You couldn't have. No one did. He was too far away from the shore. And it was too early in the morning, it was still dark.'

'But I…' No. He'd *seen* it. It was bright daylight. He'd been standing at the harbour's edge, a block from here, in Tregua. He remembered his father crying out.

He was aware that Freya had taken his hand in hers, but everything else around him was strange. Why would Anna lie to him?

'You think you saw it?' she asked.

Nico nodded.

'You were how old?'

'Five.'

'Five. You were home in bed. It was early morning, their regular fishing trip.'

'I saw it. From the harbour.'

Anna shook her head again. 'Your mother never

would have let you out of bed, let alone out of the house. You must have dreamed it. Wait.'

Anna left the room. They heard puffing and banging and she came back five minutes later with a dusty scrapbook.

'What's this?'

'In my day we kept newspaper clippings.' She flipped through the book; found the page she was looking for and opened it for him to see.

The newspaper had yellowed. It was almost thirty years old, but it was still entirely clear. Even Nico's Italian was good enough to understand the headline.

> Three missing presumed drowned off Tregua Point.

It was there, if not in black and white, at least in brown and yellow.

Anna read it aloud in Italian and he translated as she went in English, for Freya.

> 'The fishing boat is believed to have capsized off the point and all three men are presumed to have drowned in what was the biggest storm to hit Tregua in a generation.'

There'd been a storm. Not a bright, cloudless day as he'd always remembered.

'Three men? He wasn't alone?'

'No. Did you think he was?'

In Nico's memory his father had been alone. The sky had been blue.

But that memory wasn't real, he realised with a creeping disbelief that he'd ever thought it was. It was a childhood confection, a misunderstanding. Or even, as Anna had just suggested, a dream.

A dream that had become a memory.

Anna kept reading but he'd heard enough. He couldn't reconcile what he'd just learned with his own recollections; it was too confusing.

Freya took over the conversation from that point on and told Anna they needed to get going. He didn't want to argue but couldn't have even if he did. He needed to go down to the harbour. He needed to see it again.

'Come and visit me when you come back. Both of you,' Anna said.

They left Anna's cottage and he turned towards the harbour. Freya followed, understanding exactly what he was doing without the need to speak. The harbour was small, narrow, neat. An adult who was a half-competent swimmer would be able to swim from one side to the other, especially on a bright day. Now he really allowed himself to think about it, actually analyse his memory, he realised boats didn't just sink on bright days, and not in harbours as busy as Tregua's, where dozens of boats would have been at the ready to help someone in distress. Being so young he'd never questioned how it really happened.

'Do you mind if I go up to the point?' he asked.

'Of course not, but you're not going alone.'

She didn't ask if he wanted to drive and he didn't even consider asking her to stay behind.

If a part of Nico had hoped that things would become clear when they reached Tregua Point, that somehow the place would resemble that in his memory, he was disappointed. He had no recollection of ever visiting the place, a cliff that was several kilometres outside the village and only accessible by a long walking track when the road ran out. Tregua lay well in the distance, partially obscured by another headland.

'This can't have been the place,' he muttered but trusting his memory less and less.

Freya kept at a short distance, close enough if he needed her but far enough away to leave him with his thoughts. Off in the distance white tips capped the waves of the sea. Below them he could hear the roar of water crashing into the cliff.

Freya sucked in a sharp breath. He went over to her but when he saw what she was looking at he dropped to his knees.

On the ground was a small granite marker. Inscribed on it, in Italian, he could make out the date of his father's death.

The names of three men.

The worst storm in a generation.

He hadn't seen the boat sink after all.

He'd been home in bed.

Freya crouched next to him.

'I don't understand. I saw it,' he said.

He expected her to say the obvious, that he couldn't have seen it, that he was wrong, Anna was right.

'What do you think happened?' Freya asked.

'I think logically Anna and the newspaper and this plaque are right. But why is it so different in my memory?'

'I don't know. But I know that our memories are not always as reliable as we want them to be.' She smiled sadly at him.

'We can't trust any of them?' he asked.

'I'm not saying that at all. We do have to trust it, but at the same time know that sometimes our brains make us remember things that didn't happen. And sometimes it lets us forget things that did. Sometimes it does this to protect us, or to make sense of things. I don't think our memories are malicious, but as I've learned in the past few weeks, they can be affected by trauma. Your father's death was traumatic. And you were so young.'

'But why did I think I saw it?'

'Maybe you imagined it to try and make sense of it. Your imagination became your memory. Or you dreamed it and have been remembering the nightmare. I still remember some nightmares I had as a child, better than real memories. I don't know why that is.'

His memory was so strong, so vivid. Not being able to move his legs, screaming but no help coming. His father waving. It couldn't have been just a dream.

Freya touched his hand and it was so comforting he had to resist the urge to rest his head on her shoulder.

'You were five. Many people don't remember anything from when they were five at all.'

'I think I'd remember seeing my father's death.'

'Yes, but that's just it. You do remember it, so clearly. The only thing is you weren't there.'

His temples throbbed.

'I have another theory—do you want to hear it?' she asked.

He didn't want to; he sensed by her soft tone that he wasn't going to like it, but he had to hear it. He nodded.

'I think you blame yourself, not just for your father's death, but your mother's too. And of course, our accident. You're carrying a lot of guilt. So much guilt. And I don't know why, but I do know it's not good for you. And I know it isn't warranted.'

He shook his head. It didn't matter what Anna and Freya told him; he'd still played a role in all of this. It was impossible to deny it, his memories and feelings were so strong.

'Nico, you were five. How could you possibly have saved your father, even if you had been there?'

'I cry for help,' he answered, his voice cracking. He could hardly get a sound out, his throat was so closed over.

'What?'

'In my memory, I am crying for help, but no one comes. I can't yell loud enough. I can't run fast enough. My feet are stuck to the ground.'

'Like in a dream?' she asked softly.

No.

He couldn't reconcile all of this.

They were trying to tell him he hadn't watched his father die after all. That was just his own memory playing tricks on him. It was hard to erase the images in his mind of the boat sinking in the harbour with what must be the truth. Even though it never happened like that, it still felt real to him. It had been the product of his five-year-old imagination. Or maybe even a nightmare. But it hadn't happened.

'My mother had diabetes.'

'Oh, Nico.'

'Anna told me. She had several health problems apparently. That is why Anna thinks her heart gave out.'

'I'm sorry.'

'Anna says I didn't cause her death.'

Freya grabbed his hand. 'Nico, of course you

didn't cause her death. You can't have caused her illness.'

'She died of a broken heart. That's what they said.'

'Who?'

'Adults. People around us.' He didn't even know anymore who they were, only that they were older than him and knew more about the world and its strange ways.

'Nico, I don't think people do die of a broken heart, at least not years after a traumatic event. Your mother had underlying problems. It wasn't your fault.'

'But I couldn't make her better. I wasn't enough.'

He looked at her, searching for understanding in her beautiful blue eyes, hoping for her agreement. Needing her to tell him he didn't have everything wrong.

But Freya shook her head. 'I'm not a mother, but I know that if I were I would do everything in my power to stay alive for my child. Especially if he'd lost his father as well. I wouldn't give up.'

'That's what Anna said.'

'There you go.' Freya stood and brushed herself off as though it was all over, as though everything made sense.

But nothing made sense at all.

CHAPTER ELEVEN

FREYA DIDN'T SPEAK on the drive back to Monopoli and their hotel, leaving Nico alone with his thoughts. The news that he hadn't been responsible for the loss of either of his parents should have been a weight lifted from him, but instead his mood was dark.

Give him time to process it all. It's a lot to take in.

'I need a shower and a rest,' he told her at the door.

Alone.

It was implied, if not spoken, because yesterday afternoon had been a one-off. A last hurrah. They were not in a relationship and never would be. She'd practically promised him that last night.

For goodbye.

So I remember what it was like.

He didn't feel the same way about her. He cared for her as a friend, but she would never be enough to change his mind about everything else.

Freya showered as well, contemplated putting

the pink dress on again, but shoved it to the bottom of her suitcase. There was no point. Besides, now that she knew she wore it the night they'd slept together, she couldn't wear it again without obviously signalling to him how she felt about him and what she wanted.

He knows what you want, he knows how you feel and yet you're not enough.

She sat on the shared balcony and loaded the photos she'd taken that morning into her laptop. She flicked absent-mindedly through the photos of Tregua. She would have to collate them and possibly edit some before handing them over to her replacement.

They were good. Some of them were *really* good. Just looking at some of them brought all the sensations of the day back to her, the smells, the sensation of the sea air on her skin.

She was a good photographer.

A *really* good photographer.

Freya clicked on some of the other files. Unlike a few weeks ago, she now actually remembered taking these photographs, compiling the cookbooks, choosing which ones to include, everything. Unlike that time in the office when she'd picked up the cookbook and felt as though it had been written by someone else, now she *knew* she was the author and photographer. She knew she had taken these photos.

And they were good.

She was good.

Vibrant. Original. Everything that stupid editor at *The Southside Chronicle* had told her she wasn't.

Full of life. Energy. Value.

Why had she let silly words spoken by other people invade her thoughts for so long? She was a talented photographer and a brilliant food photographer. She was really good at this job she had carved out for herself with Nico.

She would find amazing work wherever she went.

But she didn't want to go anywhere else.

I want to be with Nico.

She was so lost in her thoughts she didn't realise he had joined her on the balcony until he cleared his throat. Freya jumped.

'Are you okay?' he asked.

'Fine, yes. How are you feeling?'

'Okay. Tired, I guess.' He rubbed the back of his head. He still looked thoughtful though maybe slightly less tormented.

'Nico, it's a good thing what you've found out today.'

'Is it?'

'Of course it is. Now you know that none if it was your fault.'

'Knowing is different to feeling.'

He wasn't wrong. Like the photographs in the cookbooks, she knew she had taken them, yet she didn't *feel* that she had. Nico felt guilty about his parents' deaths and it may take him some time to be able to put that to one side.

And she didn't have time.

She'd waited five years for him to want her. She couldn't wait another five. Or ten. She loved him, but she couldn't wait forever.

You're worth more than that. You deserve it all.

'It wasn't your fault.' She spoke softly even though she wanted to scream it over the balcony and the sea beyond them: *None of it was your fault and now you can love me!*

He shook his head.

'You heard what Anna said about your mother. You saw the plaque on the point. You didn't see your father's boat sink.'

He looked down.

'You don't believe any of it?'

'No, I do, but…'

'What?

'I couldn't protect *you*.'

His words silenced her words and stopped her heart.

'I can't hurt you again. I can't go through that again.' Nico looked up and straight at her. His brown eyes were wide; she'd never seen him like this. Never. He dragged his hands through his hair with such force she was almost surprised he wasn't left with fistfuls of hair in his hands.

'I watched them cut the car from around you

and pull you out. You were unconscious. I thought you were dead. And then you were asleep for so long and when you opened your eyes you had no idea who I was. None at all. You didn't even know you were in London. You'd forgotten it. Every amazing thing you'd done. You didn't know who I was. You thought I was a psychiatrist! And worst of all, you'd forgotten who you were. You were so scared, so frightened. And I couldn't help you. When I spoke to you it made things worse. I made things worse—you were terrified of me. I'll never forget that look in your eyes, Freya. I have to let you go, as much as I hate the idea. I can't stand the thought that I will hurt you again.'

Shame flushed her cheeks. She'd been thinking of herself so much these past weeks that thoughts about Nico and what he'd been going through had been cursory. She knew he was upset and worried, but this? The force of his emotions sent her reeling. Poor Nico, poor wonderful Nico. She stood on shaky knees.

'But don't you see, if you let me go, you will hurt me. Even more than the accident.' *You will devastate me. Ruin me.*

'No, you'll be fine, because you'll be safe. I can't keep you safe. I can't keep anyone safe.'

'None of it is your fault! Nico, why can't you see that?'

'I'm just trying to protect you.'

'I'm a grown woman! I can decide for myself.

Let me make my own mind up about whether I want to be hurt.'

He scoffed. 'I'm not going to hurt you. I'm not going to watch you nearly die again. I can't do it, Freya. You're better off without me.'

She closed her eyes to gather her thoughts but as she did felt pressure build behind them. No. No tears. She had to stay calm. She had to convince him.

'Nico, I'm not. And I never will be better off without you. Because I love you.'

Her throat closed over then, because she also remembered and knew in her heart that this wasn't the first time she had uttered those words to him. And if that didn't convince him, then what could?

'I love you, Nico.' Her words were rough, barely intelligible, but she could tell by the way his mouth was hanging that he had understood.

Tell me that you love me too. Tell me!

He shook his head, only slightly and only once, but it told her everything she needed to know. The bottom dropped out of her world. The Adriatic may as well have risen up to wash her away.

'I can't. I'm sorry.'

Can't? Sorry? She wanted to yell, but the tears were streaming in earnest now and all she could do was sniffle.

'Freya, my wonderful Freya, you will thank me one day for letting you go.'

She scoffed but that only propelled more tears down her face.

He's not going to change his mind. Freya recalled the rolling feeling in her stomach she'd had the night before her birthday when she told him she was considering leaving London. This was the outcome she'd always expected. She'd hoped for the other, but she'd prepared herself for this. Nico had had five years to realise how he felt about her and he hadn't decided he loved her. If the events of the last few weeks hadn't changed his mind, her standing here crying wasn't going to either.

It really was over.

What else was there to say?

She grabbed her sleeve and wiped her face.

'I'll get going then. I can move my things out of the house while you're still here. I can be gone by the time you're back in London.'

'Freya, stop. Stay. There's no rush.'

'There is. I need to move on. We both do.' And staying a moment longer would just drag things out for both of them.

She wasn't going to hang around waiting for the outcome to change when she could see now that nothing would ever change it. He was never going to change his mind.

She wasn't enough.

'Goodbye, Nico.'

She stepped up to him, lifted herself onto her tiptoes and remembered not to inhale as she touched her lips briefly against his cheek. 'Goodbye.'

She went into her room and closed the balcony door behind her.

Freya started with logistics. Changing her flight back to London. Booking a removalist. She would leave most of the furniture behind but there were some things she wanted to take with her. Some prints. And a stack of books. She would store it all in Pasadena while she figured out her next steps.

Pasadena. The thought of moving back there was not overly appealing, but it would be a soft landing before she decided where to go next.

Or would it be, as she'd always thought, a backwards step?

Go forwards, not backwards.

But right now, she was exhausted, dehydrated from all the crying and lying facedown on the bed was all she was capable of.

How had things got so messed up?

The accident, for starters.

If they hadn't crashed and her brain short-circuited at that precise moment what would have happened?

No wonder she'd gone back to the night before her twenty-fifth birthday. She'd thought of it as her brain's way of protecting her by blocking out the memory of Jane and Lachlan. Getting sacked from the job she hated. But it wasn't just that.

Her brain was also protecting her from a pain even worse than those things. It was protecting her from the reality that even though she and Nico had slept together, he never intended them to be together. That he didn't love her back. That it had all been a mistake.

No wonder she was physically fine. No wonder Nico was physically and mentally fine. No wonder the doctors were so baffled. The knock on her head hadn't been much but the news that Nico would never love her had been the real trauma.

Nico's childhood was far more complicated than she had realised even after five years of knowing him. He blamed himself for his father's death. He'd spent his life believing he'd witnessed the boat accident that killed his father, even though it was absurd to believe that a five-year-old could have saved a sinking boat.

It wasn't logical, but if he'd spent his entire life believing he had witnessed his father's death, was it really any different from *actually* seeing it?

No wonder he was so terrified about hurting her. But even now he knew that the events in his childhood were not as he'd believed, he still felt guilty about her accident.

He was never going to move past it.

And she had to accept that.

All of it.

She was leaving.

She was going to go home. It had been her plan

all along, hadn't it? That was why she'd booked the plane ticket. The accident, the amnesia, had just muddled it all up for a while but now everything was sorted.

She would leave. Build a new life without him. Make room in her heart for someone else.

She and Nico would always be friends, but with the distance between them that she needed. And so what if all she'd learned was that they were great together? That he desired her as much as she did him? So what if their bodies practically ignited when they were together?

There was so much more to relationships than great sex, deep friendship. Deep understanding, trust and connection.

So much more.

There had to be.

And she was determined to find it.

Nico picked up the car keys from where Freya had left them on the balcony table. He wasn't sure if she'd left them deliberately or not and now wasn't the time to ask. She didn't want to speak to him and it might be a while before she did again.

She'll realise it's for the best. Just give her time.

Regardless of what he'd just learned about how his parents had died, the car accident *had* been his fault. He'd been driving and too distracted by Freya to pay proper attention to what had been happening around them. And if he continued his relationship with Freya he'd continue to be distracted. And dangerous.

And if they had the family she wanted… Even in the warm afternoon sun he shivered at the thought that anything could happen to Freya's hypothetical children.

He couldn't do that. Any of it.

She needed to be with someone who could keep her safe. He wasn't that man and one day she would realise it. Maybe not immediately, but when she lived to be ninety, surrounded by a gaggle of grandkids she would thank him. The man who saved her life by letting her go.

With Freya safe in the hotel room, he decided to take a drive by himself. He drove down the coast but after a few wrong turns found himself pointed back in the direction of Tregua. The universe was telling him something. He was going back to London in a few days and he still hadn't done the one thing he really needed to do: visit his mother's old restaurant.

He had more memories of that place than any other in Tregua. It was where he had grown up, spent so many of his waking hours as a child. It was where he'd learned to run a restaurant. It was where he'd decided he wanted to be a chef.

He parked the car close to where Freya had stopped that morning, close to the waterfront but before the streets became too narrow. He preferred to travel on foot anyway; it was easier to see things and besides, he'd always walked these streets as a child. It was now late afternoon and people were emerging from their houses again after the heat of the afternoon.

He would be too early for the evening meal, but maybe they served drinks. Would he dare go in? It wouldn't be the same and he wasn't sure how he felt about that. Some things were best left as memories, but then as he'd learned today, some memories weren't real at all.

Walking along the waterfront was different now with the knowledge that this wasn't where his father's boat had sunk. He walked past bustling cafes, a few shops and then somehow reached the end of the strip without having seen his mother's restaurant.

Something wasn't right. He turned and walked back to where Via San Sebastino met the harbour and then along another three houses. The restaurant was there, except it also was not.

It was entirely different. And it wasn't just his memory. It was closed, utterly neglected. And the entire place smelt wrong. Like rotten fish.

It hadn't been cleaned in years, let alone painted. He looked in one of the windows, the glass almost too dirty with salt scum to see inside. Nico went around to the side door, where deliveries were sent. It was the door they would enter and leave from each day. He pulled and pushed on the door. It was locked, though it wouldn't have taken much to break the lock or shatter the decayed wood the lock clung to. He couldn't break and enter. He rested his forehead against the door.

As his head touched the peeling wood he remembered standing here, like this, once before. There was once a spare key. In fact, not even a spare key, but the *actual* key. Kept in the mailbox, which was also never locked. He looked to the left; it was still there. Rusted but intact. He lifted the lid and reached gingerly inside and his fingers found a single key.

No one would care if he entered. No one had cared for this building in years. The lock was a little stiff, but the door opened easily. He stepped slowly inside, inhaling the strange smells and adjusting his eyes to the dimly lit room.

The place had been sold when his mother died and he'd understood it had continued to operate as a seafood restaurant. At some point in the past twenty years, it had been abandoned. The dust was several years thick on all surfaces. The stoves remained and chairs and tables, but the pantry and shelves had been emptied. The restaurant shouldn't look like this. All his mother's work, for what? To be run into the ground? Abandoned. Unrecognisable.

It's all your fault.

A stack of menus sat on the counter. Unfamiliar. He picked one up.

Isabella's. The new owners had kept the same name, his mother's, though the menu was not as he remembered.

How is this your fault?

Because if his father hadn't died, his mother wouldn't have died and she would have continued to run the restaurant and…

His parents' deaths were not his fault. Knowing that was one thing, but shaking the feeling of it was another. Twenty years of crushing guilt was a heavy burden to simply shrug off in a single afternoon.

Besides, the car accident was his fault. His alone. He'd nearly killed Freya; he could have killed someone else.

You could fix it.

He could. He could buy it, restore it. Put in a manager. He'd have to spend a lot more time here in Puglia. He could do that; he could afford to.

He turned around to speak to Freya, to ask her opinion, but she wasn't there.

She was gone. Forever.

He buried his face in his hands.

It wasn't just this place. It was the restaurants in London. She was a part of almost everything he'd done in the past five years. He loved Freya.

He didn't want to do it without her—and not because things were better and smoother when she was around—but because he did it all for her.

He loved her.

And not just as his friend. He loved her. Body and soul. She was his person, his first thought of the morning and his last at night. He didn't want to do anything without her.

Except what if he hurt her? What if he hurt her again and this time it was worse? She was safer back in the States. Safer away from him.

Nico sank into one of the rickety chairs. Even covered in dust and grime he recognised it from over two decades ago. How could it be that his mother was long gone but the chair remained? Life's absurdities, vagaries and randomness hit him again.

Why would Freya be safer away from him, the person who cared about her more than anything in the world? She wouldn't. He may not be able to keep his loved ones safe all the time, but it was far better that they were with him, close to him, rather than on the other side of the world. Wasn't it?

Freya zipped up her suitcase and dragged it off the bed onto the floor. A car would be here shortly to take her to Bari and her flight home.

No. Not home. To London. London would only be her home for as long as it took her to pack up her things and book her next flight.

As she wheeled the suitcase out and the door to her room clicked closed behind her, she supposed she should let Nico know that she was leaving.

She'd said everything she needed to say and was sure he had as well, but five years of friendship made her pause.

She wanted things he couldn't—or wouldn't—give her. She was worth all that. She was worth everything. She was worthy of the life she wanted. Friendship, passion, success. Love.

She was worthy of it. All.

She had made this decision once; she was strong enough to walk away once and she was again now. Especially now. Nico had seen with his own eyes proof of why he wasn't responsible for his parents' deaths and yet still wasn't able to love her.

He still felt guilt over the car accident, which also wasn't right. The lorry hadn't given way. It wasn't his responsibility to take care of every other person in the world.

It was this thought that made her decide to say a final goodbye.

She knocked on the door and waited.

No answer.

She knocked again and held her ear closer to the door, listening for noise inside. There was none. She didn't have time to wait and there was, after all, nothing more to say.

She picked up the handle of her suitcase and wheeled it out.

She handed her keycard in at reception and went out to the street, now hot in the afternoon sun. The streets were quiet and her car arrived on time.

This was it.

It's time for your next adventure, she told herself as the driver lifted her suitcase into the boot and she climbed into the back seat.

The cab pulled away and she looked into the distance. *Don't think about him. Think about the future. Where will it be? New York? San Francisco?* She heard what she thought was a bang but the driver carried on, unconcerned. Then there was another.

This time it was definitely at the back of the car. She turned her head but then jerked forward as the driver braked. The driver yelled something in Italian and even though Freya's Italian was pretty much limited to food she knew it was a curse.

A bang at her window made her scream.

Then she finally saw who it was.

He was panting, sweaty.

'Stop, please,' she told the driver but there was no need. He'd pulled over and was yelling at Nico.

She rolled down her window. 'I came to say goodbye, but you weren't there,' she said.

'I want to open a restaurant. Here,' he gasped.

'What?'

'I want to reopen my mother's restaurant.'

She closed her eyes and sighed. 'That's great,

Nico, but I'm on my way to the airport. I'll miss my flight.'

'But I had to tell you.'

Her heart leapt and then crashed. Opening a restaurant in Puglia was a wonderful idea. Ambitious and it would be so much work. But what a wonderful thing to do to honour his mother and his heritage.

But it wasn't their project. It was his alone.

'Nico, I'm happy for you but I don't work for you anymore.'

'But…'

'No buts. We've been over this. I'm leaving.'

The driver held up his hands and said something else she didn't understand.

'Please leave,' she said to the driver, who then said something else and Nico spoke to him in Italian. They started to argue. The driver shook his head and began to accelerate.

As he drove away, she heard them.

The three words.

'I love you.'

She tapped the driver's shoulder. '*Arette*. Stop. Please. *Per favore*.'

Nico was at her open window again.

'What?'

'Freya, I love you.'

The driver swore again. She felt the same way. She needed to keep going or she'd miss her plane. This was the second plane ticket she'd booked to build her new life and he was getting in the way of this trip as well.

I love you.

He'd said it before. She wasn't sure when or how she knew, but she'd heard him say it before.

Maybe in a dream.

Maybe in a coma…

'I thought you were scared,' she said.

'I was wrong.'

'Let me out,' she said to the driver.

Nico took her suitcase from the boot of the car and a handful of notes from his wallet that he handed to the driver, whose face went from annoyed to delighted.

'If this is just a ploy to get me to stay… Nico, I swear…'

'It isn't.'

'You can't just say things like that.'

'Why not? It's true.'

True…

'Is it?' She loved him as well, in all sorts of ways. As a friend. A lover. A soul mate, but that didn't mean enough.

'I've never doubted that you care about me. But you know I want something more.'

'I want to give you more. I want to give you it all.'

On a warm street outside a hotel in Monopoli under the afternoon sun, Freya's heart stopped.

'You just told me you couldn't. That I wasn't enough.'

'Freya, no. You were always enough. It was me who doubted.'

'And what? You're not scared anymore?'

'No, I'm terrified. I'm terrified I'm going to fail you. But I'm more scared of not being with you. I'm more scared of letting you go.'

Her heart, her poor, broken heart began to beat again slowly. It was more optimistic than her brain, which still didn't let itself believe.

'How can you suddenly be so sure?'

'I went back to Tregua. I went to my mother's restaurant. It's been neglected.'

'And?'

'It was such a waste. I'm not sure why it is like that or what happened, but I want to rebuild it. The thought of doing it without you was overwhelming and not because of all the ways in which you help and support me but because I do everything I do because of you. If there's no one to share it with it doesn't seem worth it.'

'But you think you're going to hurt me—how will you deal with that?'

'If I let you go, I've already lost. It was something Anna said to me—I've given up before I've begun because I'm scared.'

This was a lovely speech but was he just reacting to the fact that she was about to leave?

'Nico, I want everything. A life, a marriage.

A family. And if you aren't going to be able to manage...'

'I want those things too. With you. And only with you. For the rest of our lives.' Nico picked up her hand, ran his large thumb over the sensitive skin at the base of hers. 'I love you, Freya. So much it sometimes hurts.'

And she knew. She met his eyes with disbelief but also with questions. 'The accident.'

He cast his gaze down but the pain written across his face was apparent and made her stomach drop. He nodded.

She remembered it all, the drive, him holding her hand, the feeling of pure joy that enveloped them in that car. And him saying the words *I love you, Freya. So much it sometimes hurts*. She remembered the exquisite feeling in her chest and then darkness.

'I never got to tell you that I loved you too. But I do. I love you so much. And for so long. And I realise now I'll love you forever.'

'Oh, Freya, I'm so sorry.'

'No, you've nothing to apologise for. Losing my memory made me forget all the reasons we couldn't be together and I only saw the reasons that we should.' She lifted her ankles, pushed herself up onto her toes and he ducked his head to meet her halfway. Lips met lips, souls met souls.

'You fell in love with me twice.'

She laughed. 'It's true, I did.'

'I can keep being brave and keep stepping up. Day after day, I will do my best.'

'I know you will—that's never been in doubt. You are the best man I know.'

'And Freya,' he said as he took her face in his beautiful hands. 'I will fall in love with you over and over again until the end of time.'

EPILOGUE

PEOPLE WERE RUNNING everywhere: a camera crew, the people laying out the tables and chairs, children making mischief in the chaos. He realised it had been a while since he'd seen Freya and his heart hitched but a moment later, she emerged from the restaurant, his mother's restaurant, newly painted and restored, carrying a platter to lay on one of the trestle tables.

Whose idea had it been to throw a first-birthday party so big that the entire village was invited? Oh, yeah, that's right. It had been his.

The reopening of the new restaurant had been a while coming; purchasing the site, getting the necessary approvals and then opening it had taken time. And they had both been pretty preoccupied in the meantime, first with making a television series and writing a cookbook at the same time as planning a wedding. And then busier than ever with the arrival of their first child, a daughter named Isabella.

She sat with her grandmother, and watched the preparations. Izzy was convinced the restaurant was named after her and they had done nothing to persuade her otherwise. When she was older, she would understand the significance of her name and this restaurant.

The people of Tregua had been so welcoming and positive when he'd first tentatively discussed plans to reopen the restaurant, conscious that any project with his name attached to it would bring more people and attention to their unspoilt village. But his hometown had first welcomed the film crew when he made the television series and then loved the special focus that Nico had brought to the village. Other restaurants and hotels in the area had also benefited from the increase in visitors from around the world and they proudly showed off their village.

But today, the first anniversary of the opening of the restaurant, he was open to locals only. To say thank you. And for one day, not to be Niccolò Rossetti, celebrity chef, but just Nico, local boy. Son, husband and father.

Loving Freya had been easier than he'd ever thought, and loving Izzy had at times been stressful and worrying, but overwhelmingly the most amazing part of his life. And now with a second child on the way, his heart was full.

He caught Freya's eye and she weaved her way through the crowd over to him. He held out his arm and she stepped into it.

'Are you okay?' she asked.

'I was about to ask you the same thing.'

'I'm great. And everything seems under control. I meant, how are you feeling?' She patted his chest gently. 'I meant, how are you in here?'

'Full, even though I haven't eaten.'

Her smile was radiant.

'Me too. What next?' she asked.

'Next? Next is our very special project.' He put both arms around her and rubbed her growing belly. 'And that, I think, is quite enough to be going on with.'

They had purchased a house in Tregua and planned to spend a few months a year there, at least until the children started school, to let the kids know their Italian heritage.

Freya took out her camera.

'You don't have to work today. It's a holiday.'

'I'm not working. I'm capturing memories. For you, me and Izzy. And for everyone else here today. And for this bump.'

He watched Freya, his darling, precious and amazing Freya, walk through the happy crowd, taking photos of the restaurant, the staff, the guests and most of all her mother and daughter. She circled her way back to him.

'Say "pecorino",' she said.

He laughed and the camera clicked, saving the moment forever.

* * * * *

If you enjoyed this story, check out these other great reads from Justine Lewis

Dating Game with Her Enemy
How to Win Back a Royal
Swipe Right for Mr. Perfect
The Billionaire's Plus-One Deal

All available now!